D0075505

HOW
TEACHERS
LEARN

Toward a More Liberal Teacher Education

HOW
TEACHERS
LEARN

Toward a More Liberal Teacher Education

WILLIAM A. PROEFRIEDT

FOREWORD BY MARY ANNE RAYWID

Teachers College, Columbia University
New York and London

Chapter 2 of this volume first appeared under the title "Some Thoughts about Teaching and Writing" in the *Teachers College Record*, 90(2), Winter 1985, 281–291, and is reprinted with permission.

Published by Teachers College Press, 1234 Amsterdam Avenue, New York, NY 10027

Library of Congress Cataloging-in-Publication Data

Proefriedt, William A.
    How teachers learn : toward a more liberal teacher education / William A. Proefriedt.
      p. cm.
    Includes bibliographical references and index.
    ISBN 0–8077–3359–8. — ISBN 0–8077–3358–X (pbk.)
      1. Teachers—Training of—United States.   2. Education—Study and teaching (Higher)—United States.   I. Title.
    LB1715.P76   1994
    370.71'0973—dc20   94–8960

ISBN 0–8077–3358–X (pbk.)
ISBN 0–8077–3359–8

Printed on acid-free paper
Manufactured in the United States of America

01 00 99 98 97 96 95 94   8 7 6 5 4 3 2 1

CONTENTS

Foreword by *Mary Anne Raywid*   vii

Acknowledgments   xi

Introduction   **1**

1.   Teaching as a Reflective Vocation   **7**

My First Year of Teaching   8
Reflecting on Teaching: Informal Conversations   10
Reflecting on Teaching: Formal Inquiry   12
An Alternative to Behaviorism   15
Structural Perspectives on Schooling   20
*Interpreting Schools and Classrooms: Deepening the
       Reflective Process*   21
The Conservative Ideological Shift   22

2.   Learning to Teach Is Like Learning to Write   **25**

Teaching and Writing: The Uncertain Professions   26
Technical Proficiency in Teaching and Writing   30
The Lonely Profession   32

3.   The Liberal Arts and Learning to Teach   **36**

The Current Situation in Liberal Education   38
How We Teach and Learn   40
Preparation for Teaching: The Liberal Is the Useful   42

4.   Using a Philosophical Text in the Education of Teachers   **49**

Plato's Project and Ours   50
Schooling, the Community, and Moral Education   58

5.   **Liberal Education and Responsiveness to
     Current Social Issues**   **63**

Moral Education   *65*
Multicultural Education   *71*

6.   **Methods and Student Teaching: Liberal and
     Technical Dimensions**   **79**

Teaching Questioning Techniques   *80*
John Dewey and the Problem of Methods   *88*

7.   **Only Two Cheers for Teaching as a Profession**   **94**

Knowledge   *95*
Altruism   *100*
Collegium   *103*

8.   **The Place of Teacher Education in the University**   **108**

The Development of Persons as the End of Liberal Education   *110*
The Liberal Dimension in the Professional Education Sequence   *112*
Teacher Education and the Graduate School Mentality   *115*

9.   **The Place of Schools in the Education of Teachers**   **120**

Dewey's Argument: Reconnecting Education to Life   *120*
Democratic Spaces: Decision-Making and Teacher Learning   *122*
Other Ways of Learning in Schools   *129*

10. **School–College Collaborations**   **131**

The Woods Are Burning   *132*
The Failure of Organizational Utopianism   *133*
An Argument for Smaller, Focused Projects   *137*

Afterword   **141**

References   143

Index   149

About the Author   153

FOREWORD

There are insistent demands today that education be rendered radically more effective — that schools be transformed. This book offers a direct answer to the perplexing question of "How?" It suggests that the answer lies in transforming the way teachers construe and address the challenge of teaching. And this, in turn, relates to the way they are prepared to do so.

How Teachers Learn comes at a good time. After more than a decade of effort aimed at improving schools, there is a growing acknowledgment that in the final analysis it comes down to a matter of teachers, and how they perceive and understand and relate to the teaching task. A decade ago, in the early days of our most recent (and continuing) search for Excellence, some thought school improvement was simply a matter of forcing teachers to shape up and work harder. Others advocated testing them to make sure they could pass the same sorts of exams their students were required to take. Then came efforts to entice them into more effective performance, with merit pay and differentiated statuses.

Meanwhile, other would-be reformers sought to minimize the intellectual demands on teachers by looking to curricular specifications and test-driven instruction to point them in the right direction and to keep them on track. And there have been those who looked yet elsewhere in an effort to reform education, believing that by changing the way we govern schools we could enhance teacher accountability and performance.

When the focus is narrowed to reform plans that feature the teacher as primary solution to school improvement, an ironic situation is revealed. On the one hand are those who celebrate the notion of a knowledge base that allegedly can tell teachers exactly *what* to do *when* — that is, a solid research base with algorithmic potential. On the other hand are those who insist that teaching must be rendered increasingly discretionary if it is to improve. So while the first camp is celebrating the research base that will render teacher thoughtfulness, deliberation, and discretion superfluous, the second is insisting that classroom teachers be accorded the power and wherewithal to exercise fully these qualities.

Bill Proefriedt's sentiments lie clearly with the second group: Genuinely effective teachers must have their heads on right, he says. There can be no effective substitute for their interpretation and judgment on the literally thousands of response-demanding situations teachers face each day. So reform must entail getting them to understand and go about their jobs in a new way. The first and foremost requisite is thoughtfulness: To the extent that teachers respond routinely from formulas and stock responses, they are likely to be functioning inadequately. Good teaching requires not only constant assessment of which strategies and techniques of the trade are pertinent at any particular point; it also demands a continuing awareness of the contextual connections of the matters at hand. Good teaching can emerge only from teacher thoughtfulness, in addition to content knowledge and command of technique.

The preparation teachers need is in part a matter of acquiring what we have learned about children, growth, learning—the knowledge base of teaching. It is also, of course, a matter of arriving at a knowledge of content. But what is at least as necessary is a particular intellectual stance and perspective—a consciousness and awareness and thoughtfulness about classroom events, about their connections and significance, and about the way one responds to them.

This last most essential of requisites to good teaching calls for a particular kind of preparation. It assigns a central role to liberal education, which as these pages show, plays quite a different part in teacher education than in preparation for other endeavors. A substantial part of the effort must focus not on making persons teachers, but on helping them become persons—on making them autonomous, sensitive, insightful, broadly knowledgeable, and perceiving individuals.

But it is not only liberal education that plays an unusual role in the preparation of teachers. It is also technical education that does so. For the prospective doctor or engineer, the technical knowledge acquired is a clear and unequivocal source of directives for practical application. But for the prospective teacher, Proefriedt insists, the technical knowledge base can yield no more than a repertoire of possibilities—always to be assessed in light of circumstances and context. This is not because of flaws and limitations in the knowledge base amassed to date; rather, it lies in the very nature of the teaching situation. The demands of that situation do not render technical or specialized knowledge superfluous for the teacher. But the need for interpretation and judgment and adaptation makes it necessary to focus teacher preparation to a considerable extent on the development of teachers as persons. And such a concern must suffuse the entire teacher education process. Nothing, not a single course, should be confined to sheer "nuts and bolts." Why? Because genuinely serious inquiry into nuts and bolts leads to questions about the nature and operation and purposes of the whole machine. And such matters must continually be a part of the teacher's consciousness.

This is a book about how to educate teachers. Yet it should be particularly useful to three quite different groups. First, the book's forceful argument on how to prepare teachers should be heard by those most involved with teacher preparation, as well as by those involved with setting the policies that shape it. Proefriedt makes a convincing case about how we err in our understanding of the teaching challenge, and of the negative consequences that flow from that misunderstanding.

Second, this book is an admirable entry in the dwindling genre of "public philosophy"—that is to say it is a philosophically penetrating examination of a public question, presented in terms the public can follow and appreciate. Familiar examples and an uncluttered vocabulary open the book's message to the intelligent tyro as well as to the seasoned professional. Both will be able to follow and judge the argument.

And third, because it exemplifies as well as argues the case for a certain kind of teacher education, this book would be an excellent one to place in the hands of prospective teachers—a good way of helping them understand that what they need most is not limited, as many of them believe, to a set of techniques and strategies for classroom application. Proefriedt repeatedly uses his experiences as a teacher, and those of his students, to convey the role of breadth and reflection in teaching. There are very few books on teacher education that are relevant or directly useful to prospective teachers. This is one of them.

Mary Anne Raywid

ACKNOWLEDGMENTS

I owe a debt to the many people with whom, over the years, I have talked about teaching and the education of teachers. These include former teachers of mine who first drew me into the issues I address in this book as well as secondary-level teachers, teacher educators, student teachers, and college faculty who teach courses outside the professional education sequence. Some have read and commented on sections of this book. Others have engaged in long discussions with me about their work and mine.

John McDermott introduced me to John Dewey a long time ago. Maxine Greene, Philip Phenix, and Jonas Soltis offered different approaches to the philosophy of education. Eleanor Armour-Thomas, Alice Artzt, Walter Brewer, Linda Gibson, Jim Higgins, John Lidstone, Janet Miller, June Miller, Suzanna Pflaum, Harry Rice, Jesse Vazquez, and June Zuckerman are teacher educators who, because their subject-matter and grade-level interests differ from mine, have helped to broaden my understanding of teacher education. All the members of my department have contributed to my thinking in this book. Tim Smith and Betty Sichel have talked and laughed with me in cars and at conferences over the years about philosophy and teacher education. For more than 30 years, I have talked about teaching with Bill Doherty, a former high school English teacher and administrator, who now supervises student teachers. Max Eckstein encouraged me a while back to look at teacher education in England. A PSC/CUNY grant enabled me to do that. I enjoyed long conversations about teacher education in England with, among others, Norman Greaves, Jon Lauglo, and Elwyn Thomas at the London Institute of Education; Harry Judge and John Wilson at Oxford University; and, in Scotland, David Carr at Moray House College.

Paul Longo shared his thoughts about college–school collaborations with me. Lawrence O'Connell is the student teacher I quote at length in Chapter 6. Peter Manicas (before he left for Hawaii), Edmund Leites, and Steven Steinberg are faculty members at Queens College with whom I talk about college teaching all the time and who, I think, in their different ways, are representative of what a liberal education is all about. Hayes Jacobs and the Thursday-night group at the New School for Social Research have provided just the right combination of criticism and enthusiasm for various writing efforts of mine. The librarians at Queens College were always helpful to me. Elizabeth Hennessey shared my amazement as we coaxed pages from her printer at various stages of this book's production. The editors at Teachers College Press have forced me to clarify my thinking on various points and have saved the reader from the clumsiest examples of my prose. There are many others, especially faculty at Queens College, from whose thinking I have benefited.

My adult children, Billy, Jerry, and Lauraine, enabled me to finally finish this book by ever so slowly moving out of the house. My sister has offered spiritual direction. And my grandchildren, Billy, Bobby, and Sean, now provide me with delightful distractions and with excuses for putting off future writings. My wife, Louise, served as an emergency consultant when the software with which I wrote this book placed obstacles in my path. The book is for my whole family, past, present, and future, and for all teachers, past, present, and future.

HOW
TEACHERS
LEARN

Toward a More Liberal Teacher Education

INTRODUCTION

Many teacher education reformers voice two persistent complaints about teaching today. In their opinion, (1) what goes on in classrooms today is very much like what went on there 50 or even 150 years ago—that is, no progress has been made, and (2) laypeople believe they can teach as well as professionals. The reformers' remedy for the "no progress" complaint is that teachers more thoroughly acquaint themselves with recent research into teaching practice and implement their findings in the classroom. During the last few decades, methods and findings from other disciplines have been used to systematically study the teaching and learning processes, and, reformers argue, teachers should acquaint themselves with this constantly expanding knowledge base and apply it in the classroom. Educational researchers, the argument continues, will continue to expand this knowledge base, ensuring progress in teaching practice.

To the claim that laypeople can teach as well as professional teachers, teacher education reformers respond with the argument that teaching practice is governed by an accumulated knowledge base about which laypeople are presently uninformed, and which they must master to teach effectively in today's schools. Furthermore, reformers say that the teaching profession is beginning to develop a knowledge base so specialized that it will eventually make the claims of laypeople to teaching competency seem ludicrous.

The two complaints, then, are that there is no progress and that imposters claim to do the job as well as experts. Perhaps, instead of focusing on how to eradicate these persistent phenomena, we should inquire into what they tell us about the nature of teaching and about the kind of education appropriate for teachers. In a recent work on teacher education (Clifford & Guthrie, 1988), the two complaints appear together:

> The knowledge base in modern medicine is said to double every seven years or so, posing dilemmas for medical educators. As Larry Cuban has demonstrated, a 1937 teacher would not be shocked upon entering an

1

American elementary or secondary school classroom in 1987. . . . Fundamental components of instruction have, however, generally remained the
same. Teachers still lecture and explain, students still listen (or pretend
to), take notes, use workbooks and do written assignments and (perhaps)
homework. (p. 327)

Clifford and Guthrie go on to say that one can find computers,
films, and videotapes, but no really dramatic alterations in classrooms.
They move directly from the "no progress" phenomenon to the "imposter" phenomenon.

Physicians and scientists display their shiny, "high-tech" tools and commu-
nicate in a baffling argot. Lay persons realize fully that they couldn't step
up to an operating table, jetliner flight panel, or nuclear power plant
control console and be anything less than hopelessly confused. Nevertheless, many people believe they could step into a public school classroom tomorrow and perform credibly, as well perhaps as the assigned
teacher. . . .
    In reality, teaching large numbers of students how to read, interpre-
ting complicated diagnostic test results to parents, or participating in the
legal swamp of a fair hearing requires training and experience for success.
Nonetheless, the public perception that education is technologically
weak — when stacked up against occupations such as surgery, engineering,
and architecture — coupled with the belief that almost anyone can do it,
reinforces the low status of the field. (pp. 327–328)

Note that in the formulation of each of these complaints, a comparison is made between teaching and other occupations, and that at the
heart of the matter is the worry over the status of teachers. The reformers tell us that we must respond to the complaints by altering teaching
practice, and that the way to alter teaching practice is by expanding
and disseminating the knowledge base we have accumulated about
teaching and learning.
    I will argue in this book that the view of the nature of the knowl-
edge necessary for teachers implied in this technological knowledge
base metaphor is thoroughly wrongheaded and, insofar as it has been
followed, has taken teacher education down an expensive and unprom-
ising path. Suppose that instead of responding to the no-progress complaint by pointing to the doubling of medical knowledge every seven
years and henceforth modeling knowledge for teachers on medical
knowledge, we were to consider the possibility that the knowledge and
education needed by teachers differ qualitatively from those needed by

doctors and engineers. Let us consider the possibility that the primary lever for the improvement of teaching will not be the development and dissemination of a knowledge base specific to teaching—that it will be, instead, an extension of the spirit and purposes of a liberal education into the teacher education curriculum.

If I noted shortness of breath and chest pains whenever I exerted myself, and if I were offered the choice of consulting with Galen or with a contemporary cardiologist about whom I knew little more than that she was certified and connected to a large teaching hospital, I would unhesitatingly choose the contemporary cardiologist. The inquiries made by medical science in the last 100 years have resulted in the accumulation of a body of knowledge based on correlational studies and in the development of an accurate diagnostic technology. This knowledge base and instruction in the use of the technology constitute the professional education of the cardiologist. If, on the other hand, I were asked whom I would rather study as a model of teaching, Socrates or a contemporary teacher about whom I knew only that she was certified and was connected to a school with a fine reputation, I would unhesitatingly choose Socrates. It is not likely that the cause of the lack of "progress" in teaching since Socrates' time is the failure to apply the same sort of scientific inquiry in teaching as we have applied in medicine. What knowledge might we accumulate that would enable us to teach better than Socrates? We ought, then, to consider the possibility that there are important differences between the sorts of knowledge appropriate for teachers and for doctors, and that these differences have implications for the content of and approaches to the education of teachers.

The imposter phenomenon, rather than resulting in defensive claims about the existence of a knowledge base just like those of doctors and engineers, might suggest to us a reconsideration of the nature of teaching and of preparation for it. Suppose a child of yours were about to undergo a tonsillectomy and no trained surgeons were available. A bright, enthusiastic, well-educated neighbor, who loves children and has shown herself to be sensitive to their needs, volunteers to perform the operation. She promises to read up on tonsils and surgical procedures in the next week and to consult with knowledgeable people. Next Monday, she will be at your disposal. In a second hypothetical situation, your child's teacher of earth science plans to be absent next Monday but has found a member of the community who, like the substitute surgeon, is eager and willing to stand in. The teacher has asked this person to teach a lesson about the different ways in which rocks are formed. The substitute has promised to spend the week before Monday reading about this and related topics and talking to knowledgeable people about the issue and about teaching ninth graders. Most of us could live with the substitute teacher situation, but we find the substitute surgeon idea ludicrous. Perhaps we should not assume that the sort of knowledge and education appropriate for surgeons is equally appropriate for teachers, or that, in order to make the idea of a lay substitute for a teacher as ludicrous as that of a lay substitute for a surgeon, we must accumulate and disseminate knowledge about teaching. Better to recognize the obvious differences in the sorts of knowledge and education necessary for the practice of the two professions. Many leading would-be reformers of teacher education have made a fundamental error in their choice of metaphors for the nature of knowledge useful for teachers. We need not continue on this path.

Translated into a program for the education of teachers, the scientific or medical model took this form: We need to identify the specific teaching behaviors that lead to increased student learning. The accumulated statements of such correlations between specific teacher behaviors and measurable student learning, between process and product, constitute the growing knowledge base of teacher education. But it is not enough to know that certain correlations exist. Teachers must be able to perform the behaviors identified. "Knowing that" is not enough; "knowing how" is necessary. The researchers will develop the knowledge base (that is, identify the teacher behaviors that will lead to specific pupil achievements), and the teacher educators will train the teachers in the performance of these behaviors.

This view of teacher education was surely ascendant among educational researchers in the quarter-century preceding the 1990s. Process–product research was the dominant paradigm within which researchers operated (Berliner, 1987; Dunkin & Biddle, 1974; Gage, 1978). But the approach was not confined to the research community. State education departments required that teacher education institutions file their certification programs not just as a set of course descriptions but as a list of teacher behaviors that candidates, having completed a course or set of courses, would be able to perform. If correlations between specific teacher behaviors and improvements in student learning could not be established, the teacher behaviors would be written up anyway. Competency-based teacher education (CBTE), or performance-based teacher education (PBTE), became the watchword of teacher educators throughout the country and the subject of innumerable large conferences devoted to its implementation.

This narrow view of teacher education was not new. Decades before, John Dewey had worried that "there was a tendency for every distinctive vocation to become too dominant, too exclusive and absorbing in its specialized aspect. This means emphasis upon skill or technical method at the expense of meaning" (1964, p. 208). He worried that the teacher would become merely the pedagogue. The behaviorist approach of the last few decades is the heir of a narrow, technical approach to professional teacher education that has defined education as a package of specialized knowledge and skills "at the expense of meaning." Merle Borrowman's (1956, 1965) too often neglected work documents and evaluates this tradition.

I do not argue in this book for the elimination of professional courses in teacher education; I do urge that those courses become, as they have in many cases already, more liberal in nature. They should participate in the restoration of meaning to teacher education rather than increase the emphasis on the accumulation of information and skills. The concern with meaning has always been at the heart of a liberal education, and it should be central to the education of teachers. Much of this book is devoted to visualizing professional education courses as an extension and intensification of a student's liberal education, explaining what it is about teaching that leads me to propose such an approach, and enumerating what I think is to be gained by it.

The notion that the primary knowledge appropriate for teachers, aside from knowledge of subject matter, is a collection of statements formulated from correlational studies demonstrating connections between specific teacher behaviors and enhanced student learning is now challenged by a variety of other approaches to educational research (Houston, Haberman, & Sikula, 1990; Wittrock, 1986). Research perspectives borrowed from anthropology and literature, along with those focusing on teacher self-understanding, are affecting teacher education. Nor does the content of most teacher education courses, as reflected in texts and in classroom practice, focus solely on the teacher behavior–student learning connection. Finally, many working teachers themselves are, tellingly, largely unaware of the claims of the educational researchers that a knowledge base consisting of statements about meaningful correlations between teacher behavior and student learning exists. When presented with such claims, many teachers see them as narrow formulations of what sort of knowledge and education are appropriate for teachers. Broadly educated teachers do not simply apply rules derived from the correlational studies of researchers; they actively generate complex understandings about their work based on their own perspectives and experience. Many teacher educators and teachers, then, already work largely from within a liberal model of education. I think that teacher education would benefit from a conscious reflection on the meaning and implications of that model. My book is an effort at such reflection and strives to point in the direction that a more liberal teacher education might take. I hope that both teacher educators and teachers thinking seriously about their work and education will find this volume useful.

1

TEACHING AS A
REFLECTIVE VOCATION

We teacher educators worry about what we ought to be teaching teachers, about what aspects of a teacher's work can be learned, and under what circumstances such learning is likely to occur. Since I had been an English teacher at the secondary level before I became a teacher educator, I thought I might help my inquiry into how we teacher educators ought to go about our work by asking myself what I considered to be some fundamental questions: What had I come to know as a teacher that I considered valuable? How had I come to know these things? I asked my questions with the thought that my efforts to answer them might (1) help me to plan my own teaching, (2) have policy implications for the ways in which we conceptualize and organize teacher education, and (3) help other teachers in the pursuit of their own education. Over the last few years, I have asked teachers and student teachers, in formal and informal ways, the same two questions: What have you come to know as a teacher that you consider valuable, and how have you come to know these things?

My raising of these questions was prompted by what I perceived as a dichotomy between the language of educational researchers concerned with effective teaching and the ordinary conversations of teachers about their work. It was also prompted by the long-standing and muddled argument about the relationship between theory and practice in teacher education. I never intended to compile a list of "truths" about teaching from which others might benefit. I would have scoffed at anyone handing me such a list. I did hope to identify more clearly the sort of knowledge that had proved valuable to me and to other teachers, and the conditions under which it might be acquired.

In looking at what I learned as a teacher and the situations in which I learned it, I argue for a view of teaching as a reflective vocation and urge teachers to approach their daily work in that spirit. (I hesitate to use a word such as "reflective" because it has become a part of what is at once a pious and pseudo-scientific phraseology, suggesting that reflection consists of a specifiable set of steps in which one can be trained and thereby become a reflective practitioner, and masking the reality that becoming reflective is the ongoing educational work of a lifetime.) I embed my argument in this chapter in the story of my own development as a teacher, a story that encompasses more than a third of a century and is marked by an important break after the first nine years, when I moved from being a high school English teacher to becoming a teacher educator.

MY FIRST YEAR OF TEACHING

In the spring of 1957, as I prepared to graduate from St. Francis College in Brooklyn, I applied for my first teaching job. I traveled with five fellow college students to Shirley, Long Island, to be interviewed by a school principal desperate to find bodies to place in front of classrooms bursting with children born at the end of World War II. The principal described the virtues of the Shirley school district, and I neither asked nor answered any questions. I was hired to teach a "contained" class — a straightforward enough description, since these students were not to move around from teacher to teacher, from classroom to classroom, as the other seventh-grade classes did. They were to be "contained" in one room with me, the 21-year-old new teacher, operating without the benefit of student teaching experience. The students had been placed in the class either because they had serious behavior problems or because they were slow learners, or both. I wish I could report to you how, under my tutelage, and against all odds, I brought this assortment of students together into a coherent group in which students learned skills and self-control, appreciated literature, became engaged in science projects, and were finally, to use an anachronism, "mainstreamed" into regular classrooms. But witnesses to the disaster of my first year of teaching would question my truthfulness. I lacked the technical training, the accumulated wisdom, and the strength of character needed to handle the job well.

The redeeming aspect of the experience was that it forced me to think seriously about the situation in which I found myself, and, more specifically, about ways in which it might be improved. Thus do we start to reflect on our work. Like many first-year teachers, I was preoccupied with bringing order to the classroom. I became aware of the connection between the students' capacity for learning and their emotional lives. I was overwhelmed by the content of the many different subject areas I was expected to teach, and by questions of how I might organize the learning in each of these areas so that students would benefit from their activities. I found the task of responding to the students' varied levels of ability a difficult one. The textbooks in the different subject areas tended to organize my work for me. I wondered about the relevance of the subject matter to students, about where these students were heading in life, about what sorts of things I could do in the classroom that would be most helpful to them. I wondered about my own inadequacies, my impatience, my lack of organizing ability. I wondered about the extent to which my own less than heroic efforts were nullified by the school's decision to place these children in a contained setting and inflict on them the new boy in town.

I did this wondering out loud, in the presence of older and wiser teachers such as John Quinn, Tom Mangan, and Ziggy Wielunski, veterans of World War II, as well as with Tom Young and John Flanagan, younger friends and colleagues with whom I had attended college. They listened, shared their thoughts on the issues I raised, and described problems in their own classrooms. They made suggestions about seating arrangements, about ways to teach particular units, and about how to handle individual students. We discussed subject matter and the various goals of parents, students, and teachers; we talked about the relationship of school organization to our classrooms, about the sort of town we were working in and the effect of its socioeconomic realities on school practices. We argued and sympathized with one another. The conversations took place in our daily car pool, in the teachers' lounge, and in the local pub. They were wide-ranging, unsystematic, extra-institutional, and rarely conclusive. Some of the thoughts I came away with from these various discussions I applied in the classroom, but what they mainly did was to begin to enrich my perspective on my role as a teacher. They served not as a technical education in classroom management but as an on-site extension of my general education. Learning to be a teacher turned out for me to be much like learning to be a person. In retrospect, the humor and general support of the group, the sense that others were in the same boat, meant as much to me as the specific content of our discussion. For me, teaching has never been a lonely profession.

This sort of rational discourse about teaching — a discourse shaped by everyday problems in the classroom and by concerns with educational purpose, with issues in the lives of young people that affect their capacity for learning, with reflections on one's own strengths and weaknesses as a person and as a teacher — seems a more realistic starting point for constructing a model for teacher education than the prevailing notion of a professional body of knowledge about teaching, translatable into prescriptions for teacher behavior in the classroom. (For example, teachers should have a system of rules for the classroom; teachers should call a child by name before asking a question.) Why shouldn't teacher education be a more systematic and sustained version of the sort of discourse I had in my first year of teaching and continued to have as the years passed? Why shouldn't its early stages be an effort to prepare teachers to lead reflective work lives?

A few weeks into my first year of teaching, Tom Young, the teacher of the eighth-grade contained class, and I decided to respond to the complaints of our students about their confinement. We suggested to the school's principal that we allow these students to move back and forth between our classrooms, Tom teaching math and social studies, and I science and English. We convinced the principal of the soundness of our proposal and put it into effect. We had experienced a difficulty, talked about it, planned a reasonable institutional response to it, argued for that response, succeeded, and put our idea into practice. It was a small achievement, perhaps, but it gave us a sense that we could, after reflecting on our experiences, alter not only our own behavior as teachers in the classroom, but institutional practices that impinged on our own and our students' lives.

REFLECTING ON TEACHING: INFORMAL CONVERSATIONS

In my second and third years of teaching, I taught junior high school English classes. Then for six years I taught in a senior high school. There I continued to ask questions about my work, out loud and with a new set of colleagues including Harry Wilson, John Harrington, Bill Doherty, and other teachers in the Massapequa, Long Island, district to which I had moved. We worried about our proper function in the teaching of literature. Was it simply to help the students to comprehend and appreciate the literature they read, or were we to relate the literature to the problems of everyday life? If our function was the latter, what form would such an effort take? We talked about the relationship between our teaching and our concern with civil rights issues and our country's involvement in Vietnam. We argued over which pieces of literature were most appropriate for which groups of students, and over criteria of appropriateness. We talked about the dramatic variation among students' performance and debated the extent to which our efforts could make a difference in their learning. We wondered also about the extent to which society at large and the schools' tracking system contributed to the relative performance of students. The conversations made me conscious of the rules and assumptions controlling my behavior. I was then able to change those rules and assumptions when necessary and thereby to alter the content of my daily work.

In the early 1960s we started a local of the teachers' union that now carries on collective bargaining in that district. The issue that led us to form the union local was not teacher pay but the question of providing extra time during the school day for English teachers to plan classes and to review student papers. We saw ourselves at that time as part and parcel of the civil rights movement. Individual teachers had little autonomy, and organized action by teachers was considered by administrators and school board members to be subversive of the social order. The assistant superintendent told us he believed most of the teachers would simply waste time during any on-the-job time not spent teaching a class. We learned that teachers were not trusted to oversee their own professional development, and we organized to gain some autonomy. Participation in the formation of a teachers' union local and in organized efforts to identify problems, assess possible solutions, and effect school change, provided me with new perspectives on my own role in the institution, and with the recognition that school structures and practices were not sacred and that teachers need not automatically support and enforce school policies made by others. A degree of participation in the life of the school has since seemed to me a condition for effective teacher education.

While I taught high school English, I pursued part-time a master's degree in philosophy at Fordham University. I had been a philosophy major as an undergraduate and had originally intended to teach high school English for only as long as it took me to qualify as a college teacher of philosophy. But my course work and the writing of a thesis dragged on as I marked papers, began raising a family, and participated in school politics in the districts in which I lived and worked. After I had finally completed my degree, I continued my high school teaching and also taught as an adjunct lecturer in the Philosophy Department and in the Contemporary Civilization Program at Queens College in New York City. I found the live issues of schools and teaching in the mid-1960s more interesting than my reading of Kant and Hegel. My old teacher and friend John McDermott, a philosophy professor with an interest in John Dewey and in American education, who was himself concerned with the relation of theory and practice, of thought and action, suggested that I might want to combine my waning interest in academic philosophy with my burgeoning interest in school policy and practice by doing doctoral work in the philosophy of education at

Teachers College, Columbia University. John Dewey, he pointed out, had taught in the philosophy department at Columbia and at Teachers College. I decided to take a course in the philosophy of education at Teachers College and see how I liked it.

REFLECTING ON TEACHING: FORMAL INQUIRY

The course I took was Phil Phenix's "Ways of Knowing," and Phenix offered me a scholarship and family stipend to finance my doctoral work. I withdrew my retirement money, secured a loan, continued to work in the evening at Queens College, and was able to do a year of full-time graduate work at Teachers College. I now did in a more formal fashion what I had already been doing for eight years: reflecting seriously on my work as a teacher, and thinking more generally about the problems of schooling in America. At Teachers College, Jonas Soltis introduced me to some British philosophers of education who had been much influenced by A. J. Ayer and the logical positivists. D. J. O'Connor (1966), for example, saw philosophy as an activity of criticism and clarification, found it logically absurd that we should expect demonstrations of how we should live, found the problem of how we were to go about making value judgments unsolved, and thought it a more modest and wiser enterprise to scrutinize the puzzling features of value statements than to attempt to develop comprehensive educational philosophies of the sort offered by Plato and Rousseau.

My reactions to the British and American analytic philosophers of education were mixed. I found some of them, at least, offering rather thin intellectual soup. My own training at Fordham in the history of philosophy allowed me to see the ways in which thinkers like O'Connor too easily and arrogantly dismissed the efforts of philosophers of the past to link questions of educational aims and practices with their inquiries into the nature of man and of the good society. At the same time, I was drawn to these thinkers' striving for clarity, to the plainspokenness and the taste for homely examples that characterized their writing. I thought then and still do that the analytic style had much to offer the discourse about education, which too often went on in a well-intentioned but muddled fashion.

I was especially impressed by the force and clarity of Israel Scheffler's (1965) work in distinguishing the concept of "education" from a variety of other ways of influencing peoples' behavior, and found the argument over the concept of "indoctrination" engaged in by a number of philosophers of education both fiercely intelligent and relevant to the discussions I had with other teachers about how to handle the controversial issues of war and racism in our classrooms.

I did wonder if some of my fellow teachers would be willing and able to attend to the bravura performances engaged in by these thinkers. I suspected a dichotomy between the language of the philosophers and the immediate interests of classroom teachers. The philosophers, like other educational thinkers, sometimes took refuge behind the parent discipline and employed an unnecessarily abstruse idiom. On the other hand, some teachers struck me as intellectually lazy and impatient with discussions that had no immediate pay-off in the classroom. The gap between intellectual inquiries into educational problems and teachers' interest in these issues is the continuing and intractable scandal of teacher education. Bridging the gap is made harder by the fact that one of the longstanding criticisms of the type of knowledge purveyed to teachers in education classes is its banality and its lack of analytic seriousness. The task, of course, is to develop a discourse that will be perceived by teachers as both intellectually sound and relevant to the daily work of classrooms. This task will require that serious inquirers into educational issues show clearly connections between their inquiries and the world of teaching and that they describe their work in a language accessible to teachers. From teachers, it will require a new intellectual seriousness that will allow them to appropriate the language of the scholars into their own conversations and to reject the banalities offered to them in multimedia in-service kits purchased by administrators looking for the answer to their teacher development problems.

Besides the difficulty of connecting their language to the experience of teachers, the analytic philosophers proclaimed the futility of all talk about educational aims and values. I had modest enough expectations for the impact of rationality on the political arena without embracing a philosophical position that questioned the very possibility of rational discourse about the great value choices of the society. I knew that underneath much of the contemporary educational debate, and much of the conversation I engaged in with other teachers and with members of the school district in which I lived, lurked Socrates' questions about the nature of the good life and the good society. I also knew that the sorts of classrooms we ran and the kinds of educational systems we built were in fact our answers to those ancient questions. I thought there were better and worse ways to address those questions, a position subscribed to by the more thoughtful of the analytic philosophers, and that, however modest our impact might be, we ought to get on with the inquiry.

At their most astringent and arrogant, the analytic philosophers insisted that only two sorts of claims about knowledge made sense: statements whose predicates were already contained in the subject (for example, about the famous triangle the three sides of which we can safely predicate) and empirical statements the truth of which could be verified (Ayer, 1936) or, in Popper's (1959) formulation, falsified (in the case of the assertion of causal laws). Many of the faculty in the various departments at Teachers College reflected this positivist approach. This was especially true of the psychologists focusing on learning theory and on testing and measurement. The concern with careful data collection, with efforts to show correlations between educational and societal variables, began to define the practice of the various social science perspectives on education offered at Teachers College and at the other major research institutions involved in educating educators (teachers, the faculties of teacher education institutions, and the growing corps of administrative and other specialists in the schools). The empiricism was, of course, linked to institutional efforts to apply the disciplinary perspectives of the various social sciences to teacher education.

The shortcomings of this empiricism, pointed out in the extraordinarily sophisticated analyses of social and educational research of the 1970s and 1980s (Bernstein, 1978, 1983; Bredo & Feinberg, 1982), should not obscure the extent to which the arrival of the social science disciplines on the educational scene represented a breath of intellectual fresh air when compared to the general mush, slogans, and unexamined assumptions and claims that too often passed for educational thinking in the first half of this century. My own reflections about schooling and society in America benefited greatly from the questions and perspectives introduced by philosophers, historians, and social scientists. Much of this new work fed into the sorts of issues I had discussed with my teacher colleagues and broadened my ability to think about issues that, I was convinced, were pertinent to lives in classrooms.

In educational psychology, the professors were defining learning, in what I perceived as a dogmatic and tendentious fashion, as changes in student behavior brought about by the manipulation of variables by the teacher. The behaviorist method had become a metaphysics. Not only was observed behavior the only thing we could measure, but talk about other ways of conceiving knowledge was banished as unscientific nonsense. The existence of the mind in the machine was denied, and hundreds of years of philosophical psychology were shunted onto a historical siding.

The appeal of behaviorism for teacher education and for educators in general lay not only in its argument for an empirical human science but in its promise to enable teachers to understand the patterns of children's learning and to intervene at appropriate points in the patterns to ensure student learning. Behaviorism not only presented itself as a method of inquiry into the learning process, it dangled the promise of a technology of teaching. I began to speculate on how nicely the behavioral approach to education, and more specifically to the education of teachers, tied in with certain themes in the larger culture within which the schools operated, and with the significant role that the schools had been carving out for themselves within that culture. My speculation on the cultural context of the behavioral approach to teacher education and my reflection about my own learning as a teacher have led me to reject the claims of the behaviorists to an exclusive method of inquiry in educational research and their efforts to monopolize teacher training and school and classroom management. I will now elaborate on my speculations and try to elicit from the narrative of my work as a teacher and a teacher educator a criticism of the behavioral approach, an argument for an alternative view of knowledge about teaching, and a proposal for an alternative set of assumptions from which we might develop a more effective teacher education.

AN ALTERNATIVE TO BEHAVIORISM

Historically, we Americans have championed a view of knowledge that rejects the purely theoretical life and have elevated the practical and utilitarian. Our political genius has been a practical one, contributing no great ideology or political theory, but inventing and sustaining workable institutions that adjust themselves to a variety of internal interests and external conditions. Our "official" American philosophy of pragmatism has emphasized the concrete consequences of ideas and has judged their worth by the extent to which they enable us to shape our experience, serving us as instruments in the struggle of life. We have celebrated the interaction of human intelligence with the world around us and the active role of that intelligence in shaping the world. "The world stands really malleable," William James (1981) told us, "waiting to receive its final touches at our hands" (p. 115).

We were known in the nineteenth century not for our theoretical science but for its engineering applications—the building of our bridges, railways, and canals. We had all along a confidence in our capacity to shape and control the world around us. At times that confidence expanded into arrogance. Listen to Emerson: "Nature is thoroughly mediate. It is made to serve. It receives the dominion of man as meekly as the ass on which the savior rode" (quoted in McQuade, 1981, p. 22).

It's not surprising that we viewed the schools in this country as shapers of the individual and of society. Starting with the rejection of the notion that a natural order of things was reflected in the existence of hereditary social classes, we saw the schools as engines of social mobility and guarantors of social order. We used them to Americanize immigrants, teach morality and road safety, reduce alcoholism and drug dependency, and relieve other problems faced by society. The schools picked up the action-oriented, practical-application view of knowledge present in the culture. They were ripe for a behaviorism that promised a technology of teaching rooted in scientific laws of human behavior. There were students to be shaped, a society to be built.

In Skinner, educators found the belief that we need not inquire into or argue over ends, that we are already in possession of a set of shared assumptions about the good life, or the ends of education (1967, p. 159). Others claimed neutrality about ends, insisting they were offering only a technology to move students in whatever directions the school authorities determined were worthwhile. In general, the behaviorists contributed to the sense that some of the analytic philosophers had created — that rational discourse about educational and societal ends was either unnecessary or impossible. In education as in the larger culture, our technological capacity, our great American know-how, outstripped our capacity to reflect along the way on the ends toward which we were moving.

An examination of educational ends is simply not a part of the discourse of most teacher educators and school administrators who operate within the behaviorist framework. Too often behavioral learning theory is taught in classrooms as *the* scientific approach to learning and is not examined critically. (The "humanistic" teacher educators are, of course, guilty of the same sort of indoctrination as regards their approach.) At other times, the behavioral theory is simply the unexamined basis of a practical teacher training program in which teachers are trained to engage in particular behaviors claimed to lead to increased learning on the part of their students. In schools, teachers are asked to formulate their aims in terms of specific student behaviors that they can observe and document. They are rarely encouraged to evaluate critically the theoretical assumptions and claims embedded in the practices they are asked to adopt.

The behavioral-empiricist mode of research continues to be the dominant one in education, although it has been much criticized, although other models of inquiry claim adherents, and although some of its practitioners now proceed in a more sophisticated and less dogmatic fashion. In the late 1970s, N. L. Gage's *A Scientific Basis of the Art of Teaching* (1978) recapitulated the behaviorial-empiricist position. Gage seemed to take a reasonably modest stance when he wrote that he did not speak for a science of teaching that implied that "good teaching will some day be attainable by closely following rigorous laws that yield high predictability and control" (1978, p. 18). He said that he spoke only for a scientific basis for the art of teaching. He compared this art/science relationship to the situation in engineering and medicine. He pointed out that physicians have in the twentieth century a scientific basis for their work in the relationships that have been established among such variables as red blood cell count, blood pressure, and respiration rate. The physician, Gage wrote, uses this scientific knowledge in an artful way as he treats each patient. The artistry enters when the physician (or engineer) determines "when to follow the implication of the laws, generalizations and trends, and, especially when *not* to, and how to combine two or more laws or trends when solving a problem" (1978, p. 20). Similarly, artful teachers would be called on to apply their knowledge of the impact of a teacher behavior variable such as "criticism" on such factors as the performance and anxiety levels of pupils.

The scientific basis for the art of teaching of which Gage speaks consists of our knowledge of "regular, non-chance relationships in the realm of events with which the practice is concerned" (1978, p. 20). There are, Gage writes, numerous types of variables that interest social scientists studying education. They look at teacher characteristics such as age, socioeconomic status, and educational background; at context variables such as class size and type of community; at process variables, that is, the specific behaviors of teachers and students as they interact with each other; and, finally, at product or outcome variables, that is, various measured learnings. Teachers, parents, and administrators, Gage tells us, care most about process–product relationships. They want to know whether some teacher behaviors are demonstrably better in terms of product variables, that is, student learning, than others. "If the answer is yes, we have a basis for improving teaching and the training of teachers. If the answer is no, we are left without a scientific basis for the art of teaching. Then every teacher must use his or her personal common sense, intuition, insight, or art with no guidance from any relationships or regularities that may have been laid bare through scientific methods" (1978, pp. 23–24). The poor state of teacher education is due in large part, for Gage, to the insufficiency of the

scientific basis he has described, that is, to an insufficiency in established correlations between specific types of teacher behavior and increased student learning.

I think Gage errs in limiting the "science" of teaching to the collection of regular non-chance relationships between variables. The term
confers a special status on such statements and sets them off from statements that illustrate, in Gage's formulation, intuition, insight, common
sense, or art—clearly, in his eyes, less desirable ways of looking at
school realities. Gage does not see the "something else" beyond the
scientific as part of a public, rational discourse deserving of inclusion in
the study of education.

Many teachers and teacher educators resist efforts to develop a
technology of teaching. Throughout schools and teacher education institutions one can find, gathering dust on shelves, pages of statements
about what behaviors students will be able to demonstrate after they
have completed a particular unit or course. Teachers continue to resist
directives to place expected behavioral outcomes on blackboards at the
beginning of their lessons; they continue to fight districtwide efforts to
impose curricula and testing programs based on behavioral principles.
It seems to me that we are all exhibiting a dumb sense that the project
of teaching in which we are engaged is quite different from the one
defined for us by the behaviorists. According to the application model
of the relationship between knowledge and teaching practice, a teacher's educational development would consist simply of a growing ability
to identify specific teaching behaviors — for example, "praise" or "higher-
order questioning"—that have been shown empirically to elicit increased learning in children, and of the practice of these behaviors in
classrooms.

Now there is much worthwhile in the identification of such behaviors, in the scientific support given to them, in reminders to teachers of
their efficacy, and in efforts to habitually employ them in classrooms.
But surely the knowledge derived from this process–product approach
is only a small part of what should constitute the education of a teacher.
If only education and the other great human endeavors yielded to such
a technical fix! What is needed, instead, is a commitment to a lifetime
of sustained reflection with other teachers on the work at hand. At the
heart of that reflective effort are an inquiry into questions of educational purposes and an effort to align what and how we teach with
those purposes.

Gage's emphasis on process–product research in classrooms dimin-
ishes the significance of the influence of the larger structures of the
society on student learning; his methodological focus on small-scale

variables rules out a contextual understanding of the real life of schools and classrooms. This context, it seems to me, is often present in the most thoughtful teacher conversations. When we discuss what constitutes a worthwhile learning experience for a particular student, we begin to raise the broadest and most serious questions about the individual and social purposes of schooling. Curriculum choices, grading practices, the placement of students, coping with disorderly students—all issues in which the average teacher is involved—require us to place classroom situations in broader contexts and to recognize that the education of teachers cannot be confined to the study of teaching variables and training in their implementation.

Scientific and engineering analogies mislead us in our effort to understand the relation between knowledge and teaching. They define the relationship between knowledge and activity as one in which the individual teacher dips into a cache of scientific laws, artfully choosing the right ones for the right circumstances. Such is not the connection between knowledge and activity that I have experienced in my own growth as a teacher.

My sense is that my education as a teacher has taken place in much the same fashion as my education as a person. Neither has been a matter of the learning and application of laws to the situation at hand; both have involved an immersion in formal and informal discussions. The relationship between knowledge and practice has been less the applica-tion of discrete pieces of knowledge to classroom teaching than an irreg-ular back-and-forth movement in which I raised questions about my own teaching practice, shared the questions with others, found oblique references to them in my readings or formal classes, discovered inepti-tudes in my own practice of which I had been unaware, changed and changed again my approaches in classrooms, and altered my perspec-tive on educational methods and practice. My own growth in the un-derstanding necessary to function as a teacher is simply not captured by the notion of the learning of truth statements by teachers and their artful application to classroom situations.

Nor was I thrown back entirely on my own intuitions and insights. I engaged in rational discourse within a particular community of teach-ers, and that conversation was broadened through formal course work and reading. The knowledge I have found useful as a teacher appears to be an extension of wider knowledge, and of habits of inquiry usually associated with the concept of a general or liberal education, which locates problems within wider contexts, encourages critical reflection (especially on questions of purpose), and provides each of us with a perspective on our daily life. The alternative to an education for teachers based on an oversimplified natural science model need not be idio-syncratic or irrational. It can consist of teachers themselves, in formal and informal ways, in schools and in universities, forming a community of rational discourse about teaching.

STRUCTURAL PERSPECTIVES ON SCHOOLING

During the 1970s, I taught a graduate course at Queens College in which I asked teachers to read Bowles and Gintis's *Schooling in Capitalist America* (1976), Jencks's *Inequality* (1972), and Michael Katz's *Class, bureaucracy, and schools: The illusion of educational change in America* (1971). These authors saw the schools as standing at the center of the false promise of American society. They saw the schools' promise to help the poor move into the social and economic mainstream as diverting energy from the more fundamental task of bringing the centers of economic power under democratic control. They described the schools as places in which students were convinced of the "rightness" of their assigned level within the economic hierarchy. Through advisement policies, tracking, standardized testing, and other practices they were prepared to take their places within a hierarchically ordered work force; the school inculcated the attitudes and the skills necessary for the running of the capitalist economy.

This sense of the schools' function represented an extraordinary challenge to the mainstream belief that individuals, through their own energies, drive, and motivation, were pursuing happiness and moving up the social ladder, and that the schools were at the center of all of this dynamic movement. Teachers saw their own lives and work as important insofar as they were helping others to follow the dream. The socialist critics, of course, did not accept the notion that the acquisition of the cognitive skills the schools purported to teach determined the individuals' place in the social and economic order. Jencks pointed out that there was no causal relation between school expenditures and cognitive skill levels. Bowles and Gintis (1976) traced income differences in the society, not to individual abilities on which teachers and schools might have some effect, but to "the property and power relationships that define the capitalist system" (p. 12). In this view, not only did schools fail to contribute significantly either to social mobility or to income equality, they also fostered skills and forms of consciousness dictated by the needs of existing capitalist structures. Bowles and Gintis dismissed the meritocratic justification for the hierarchical division of labor as the rationalization of privilege by the ruling class.

I read these books and others like them with a large number of teachers in my various graduate classes over a period of about 10 years. Some few students essentially agreed with the analyses they read, and yet sought ways to find meaning in their everyday work as teachers. Some found any analyses that looked at the relationship of schools to larger issues in the society simply irrelevant to their day-to-day classroom problems. Finally, some teachers were grievously offended by the critique; it challenged their most basic social beliefs and questioned the significance of their work. My own conclusion (Proefriedt, 1980, 1981) was that these authors had issued a welcome challenge to the focus of educational research on teacher variables and student learning, but that they, particularly Bowles and Gintis, had embraced a reductionism that failed to allow any room for human agency within the structural framework described.

During the 1980s American Marxists with a special interest in education began decrying a vulgar Marxism, which reduced all social explanation to economic determinism. There emerged within Marxist intellectual circles a rejection of reductionism, a new emphasis on the interaction of various forces in the society, a recognition of the importance of human agency and of the relative autonomy of various institutions within the society, including schools, and a denial of any historical teleology (Isaac, 1987). Hence a new literature has developed that speaks of teachers engaging in an emancipatory, critical activity and contributing to the transformation of individuals and society. This literature, it seems to me, shows extraordinary promise insofar as it reminds teachers of the larger social situation in which we find ourselves, while it asserts an active role for them in helping students to grow as individuals and as critical participants in society.

INTERPRETING SCHOOLS AND CLASSROOMS: DEEPENING THE REFLECTIVE PROCESS

In tandem with the socialist criticism of American education, a broader criticism of the social sciences grew louder during the 1970s and 1980s, raising questions about the possibilities and limitations of such inquiry. This criticism had an especially dramatic effect on research into education. Both empiricist classroom process research and research into broader context variables, such as parental income and level of education, came under criticism. The idea that human behavior could be subsumed under causal laws was questioned. In education especially, the disenfranchised were the population likely to be studied in the empirical mode. Some insisted that the meaning of people's lives escaped the claimed correlations.

Kuhn's (1962, 1977) descriptions of the manner in which scientific paradigms came to be and passed away emboldened educational researchers and others to explore new ways of examining human behavior. Philosophers, looking at the social sciences, pointed out that no deductive theoretical systems had been developed. What had been developed were isolated statements summarizing observed uniformities in relationships among variables, and some educational researchers questioned whether we had established even such isolated relationships (Gage, 1978, pp. 24–27). Much was made of the naiveté of empirical researchers who failed to see the ways in which their conceptions, questions, and methodology mediated the raw data, or real world, that they saw themselves studying. There was a general reaction against the belief that the natural sciences offered a model for the human sciences. The notion of a different logic appropriate to the understanding of human behavior, one that included attempting to understand actions from the point of view of the meanings and purposes assigned to them by the actors, took hold and was perceived as an alternative to understanding human behavior in terms of interrelated empirical regularities. Hermeneutics, or the interpretation of social realities, including life in schools, as texts requiring an understanding of local norms and meanings, became an alternative paradigm of inquiry (Erickson, 1986). The mind was put back in the machine as researchers tried to understand the purposes embedded in human behavior. The educational ethnographers, like the historians and the philosophers and some of the earlier social scientists, seemed to me to offer a systematic extension of the ways in which intelligent teachers inquire into the realities of school life.

THE CONSERVATIVE IDEOLOGICAL SHIFT

In the late 1970s and early 1980s, an ideological shift occurred in this country. A number of educational reform documents reflecting the new conservativism appeared (National Commission on Excellence in Education, 1983; The Twentieth Century Fund, 1983). They were offered in the context of a concern with national security and economic preeminence, and with individual competitiveness in a complex urban society. They called for stricter standards for promotion and graduation, a more coherent course of study, and an orderly learning environment, and, in some cases at least, they exhibited a renewed interest in educating to inculcate character and citizenship. They called for adequate homework assignments, more student time on task, and the increased use of standardized testing to determine student progress. Once again, educational discourse, whether engaged in by teachers or by laypeople, took its cue from the larger political setting within which the schools operated, and teachers wishing to engage intelligently in that discourse had to be aware that they were arguing not only over a set of scientific claims about education, but about the larger political issues of the day as they manifested themselves in the schools.

In 1986, the U.S. Department of Education published *What Works: Research About Teaching and Learning* (1986). The title was an appealing one to teachers in my classes who wished to find out how to be effective in their classrooms. The "findings" in the pamphlet were presented as having the authority of research science. In his introduction to the pamphlet Chester Finn told us, "We included only those findings about which research evidence and expert opinion were consistent, persuasive, and fairly stable over time" (p. 1). The report claimed to offer discrete findings about teaching and learning, culled from empirical research, but its subtext was a set of ideological claims buried, often not so deeply, in what seemed to be only claims about "how" one could most effectively carry out the educational process. We learned, for example, that "What parents do to help their children learn is more important to academic success than how well-off the family is" (p. 7). We were then offered a list of helpful things that parents might do such as "provide books, supplies, and a special place for studying, [and] observe routines for meals, bedtime and homework" (p. 7). Parents were also told that they could improve their children's chances for success by "emphasizing the importance of education, hard work, and responsibility, and by encouraging their children's friendships with peers who have similar values. The ideals that students, their parents, and their peers held," we were assured, were "more important than a student's socioeconomic and ethnic background in predicting academic success" (p. 17). Throughout the document, claims were made that research supported the significance for academic achievement of hard work, self-discipline, and personal responsibility on the part of students, along with high expectations from teachers.

The pamphlet contained many helpful suggestions about questioning students and assigning homework, and about teaching reading, writing, science, mathematics, and foreign languages. The whole work, however, was offered within an ideological context that downplayed the significance of economic factors in student achievement. With its use of a language of personal responsibility, it found a ready audience among many teachers; at the same time, few who welcomed this emphasis could accept the notion that the conditions of poverty suffered by many children in this country were not likely to have a significant effect on school achievement and later life. The "common sense" of the document was, in fact, a hidden ideology that appealed all too easily to teachers looking for concrete suggestions and impatient with the notion that educational efforts by schools and families must be accompanied by, and not offered as an alternative to, large-scale efforts to eliminate glaring inequities in society.

My own experience as a teacher and teacher educator has led me to better understand the nature of the knowledge that teachers develop and use, and of the ways in which they acquire it. It seems that the sort of knowledge teachers find most useful in their work emerges within informal friendship structures and is transmitted within a context in which they share their difficulties and provide reciprocal support. This knowledge appears to be an extension of that wider knowledge, usually associated with the concept of a liberal education, which locates problems within wider contexts and provides individuals with a critical reflective capacity and with a perspective on their daily lives. Whether teachers are linking larger social changes with classroom realities or responding critically to ideologically skewed research, they are exhibiting a view of teacher knowledge that is active and constructive. This notion of knowledge stands in contrast to the idea of a science of education that rests on correlations between teacher behaviors and student performance and expects teachers to learn the behaviors and practice them in the classroom.

The confidence I had in my understanding of teacher knowledge, arrived at by reflection and by listening to working teachers, was supported by the variety of new approaches to inquiry in education that emerged in the late 1970s and the 1980s. But the behaviorist-scientistic approach had the advantage of being rooted in a powerful, persuasive, and, too often, unexamined metaphor. Teachers, like doctors, could dip into a scientifically generated knowledge base, in this case one consisting of statements about non-chance connections between specific teacher behaviors and student learning. Education, like the medical profession relying on a growing body of scientific research, would make progress. Too many teacher educators were trapped in this scientific metaphor of knowledge. We needed a new understanding of teacher knowledge. We needed a new metaphor.

2

LEARNING TO TEACH IS LIKE LEARNING TO WRITE

At the same time I was looking in a sustained fashion at questions about the education of teachers, I decided to try my hand at fiction writing. I therefore enrolled in a workshop run by Hayes Jacobs at The New School for Social Research in New York City. I initially saw the workshop and fiction writing as a vacation from my work in teacher education. Then it dawned on me that reflecting on the educational experience I was going through with the other students in that writing workshop could help me to better understand the ways in which teachers learn to teach. I began to ask myself questions about the similarities between learning to write and learning to teach.

The people in the workshop came with a clear purpose. No one was there to fulfil certification requirements. No one was without a knowledge of the basics of written expression. We were there to learn more about how to write fiction. We wanted to publish. The focus was on our own work. Most class time was spent in the reading and discussion of student manuscripts, although the instructor usually spent part of the session making more general comments on writing.

The instructor was a practicing writer. The students' knowledge of his background contributed to their trust in his direction. More importantly, his own continuing writing experience lent a richness and concreteness to his comments. His being a writer was a necessary but clearly not sufficient condition for the effective work he did with our group. He also had an abiding interest in the workings of his own craft as evidenced by his familiarity with autobiographies and biographies of writers, especially with passages in which writers talked about their own work habits, sources of inspiration, or overcoming of some technical problem. Further, he took a genuine delight in the best efforts of the class members, reading them aloud and commenting on them. He spent enormous amounts of time reading and making detailed comments on the completed short stories that we turned in.

25

TEACHING AND WRITING:
THE UNCERTAIN PROFESSIONS

Many have said about both teaching and writing that it is impossible to identify clear and specific criteria for what constitutes a successful effort in either field. Some critics argue over the merits of a particular book. Others argue over what criteria should be employed in settling such disputes. Still others raise questions about the very possibility of formulating such criteria. How then can we teach people to become good writers? This is not unlike the situation in teaching.

Consider how differently A. S. Neill, were he alive, and E. D. Hirsch might react to the efforts of the same teacher. Because these critics think differently about the nature of subject matter, about human freedom and purpose, about educational ends, and about a host of other issues that impinge on the way in which they would formulate a notion of what constitutes a good teaching effort, they would undoubtedly disagree on ways to educate good teachers. At a more mundane level, in some quarters we find the strict teacher praised for bringing order into a chaotic classroom and in other places condemned for instilling fear in his students. The charismatic, brilliant lecturer may be praised by some for inspiring an audience, and dismissed by others for focusing too much on her own performance and too little on her students.

A sound teacher education will address the normative question of what constitutes good teaching. Good teachers, like good writers, develop criteria for good teaching as they go. In neither case does one embark on a road with a destination clearly in mind. But one does embark. One begins to work, and to reflect on the nature of the work, without being able to specify exactly what constitutes good teaching or good writing. For both the teacher and the writer, the reflection is embedded in more immediate tasks. The very getting on with the work can be part of the process of understanding what it means to do the work well. This uncertainty about what constitutes good writing or good teaching suggests that the sort of knowledge one acquires in becoming a teacher or a writer and the way in which one acquires it cannot be subsumed under the standard notion of a preexisting body of knowledge being acquired by entrants to a profession and then applied to their daily work.

Let us see whether the advice given to fledgling writers is similar to that offered to teachers. In my workshop, the instructor presented us with a list of the qualities usually present in a good short story. Before I reproduce the better part of that list, let me describe the context in which the list was offered. The instructor had emphasized from the beginning that in his course we would be getting one point of view on writing, and a set of comments on our own writing rooted in that point of view. He underlined his wish that students in the class not take his comments as the final word, but that we reflect on what he had to say, and seek other perspectives. He told stories of now-well-thought-of novels that had been turned down by slews of editors because of perceived inadequacies. This recognition of dramatic differences of opinion among the "experts" did not lead him to a wishy-washy approach in the advice he gave us. He played his own game with a fairly commonly accepted set of rules, and a few uncommon ones, and he played with enthusiasm and attention to detail. But he bracketed his own game within the recognition that one could sometimes break some of the rules and still carry off the game successfully, and, further, that there were other games being played in the neighborhood, with different sets of rules, that some of us might want to take a look at. In short, his advice was rooted in his own beliefs about what constituted good writing, but was offered in a context that encouraged an active and reflective challenge to his approach; the people in his class were to test whatever was said there in the larger context of their own reading, their conversations with others, and finally their own writing experience.

Now to the list. According to it, a good short story had a strong central character caught up in a crisis; a single, unified point of view; a limited time span; a significant theme; strong conflict dramatically portrayed, usually through generous use of dialogue; emphasis on the actual, not the typical; a distinctive sense of geographical place; vital minor characters subordinated to the main character; a length appropriate to the story's complexity and to a reading at a single sitting; and a steady forward movement of a story line arranged to provide maximum suspense.

Such a list is easily dismissed. One can point to well-regarded stories that do not exhibit all or even most of the criteria on the list. One can say the list is banal, or that good short stories are not written by following such lists, or that most of the requirements are too general to be helpful for a specific writing task. All of these disclaimers were in fact made by the instructor, along with his concern lest we see the list as a set of directions to "apply" when we wrote our next short story. As far as I could see, no such admonition was necessary. We went on writing our stories, forgetting the items on the list except when one of them would pop into our heads as we were writing or rewriting a story: "Look at what I'm doing here, telling how this fellow typically acted instead of plunging the reader into the actual events of my story. That would be so much better. Now I've switched the point of view here, but that switch is crucial to the conflict of the perceptions of these two people, and that conflict is the whole point of my story. And it is my story. I'll go with it."

The rules provided us with a vocabulary, a conceptual structure within which we were able to reflect on our work and to discuss it with others. But the vocabulary learned in class was digested into a larger vocabulary and culture that had developed around our common task of writing fiction. We argued about these matters, with the instructor and among ourselves, as we wrote. The rules I outlined above and a thousand others offered by the instructor, picked up in writer's guides, or developed from our analyses of what favorite writers were doing—all contributed to a language in which we could reflect on and revise our work.

In teacher education, rules are too often perceived quite differently. Teachers are told there is a scientific basis for the art of teaching, consisting of identified teacher behaviors that have non-chance relationships with desirable learning behaviors. But since so many variables are involved in student learning, even those who, like N. L. Gage (1978), champion the notion of a scientific basis for the art of teaching, recognize that sometimes the teacher as artist must step in and make clinical or artistic judgments about the best ways to teach (p. 20). Gage and others, however, still resort to medical or engineering analogies as they talk about the application of a knowledge base to teaching practice, and they characterize the task of teacher education as a dissemination of that knowledge base and the teacher training process as a movement from knowing *that* to knowing *how*.

Up until a few years ago the orthodox literature on teacher education was dominated by this aspiration toward the scientific. (That stance has mellowed lately, and the doors have opened widely on questions about what constitutes appropriate method and content in research about teaching and schools, about what sorts of knowledge teachers need, and about the nature of their relationship to that knowledge.) One can search far and wide in writing about writing and still not find this scientific aspiration. Writers know they are going about quite a different task than doctors or engineers, and they exhibit no desire to model their work on the scientific professions. They do work terribly hard, nevertheless, at the business of becoming better writers.

Add to this scientific aspiration the understandable but nevertheless pernicious desire of so many teachers for explicit directions for carrying out their teaching practice, and the willingness of too many teacher educators to provide them with just such directions, and we have set up a skewed context in which teachers are kept from genuine inquiry into their work. Teachers, like writers, it seems to me, need to look at the "rules" of teaching as possible additions to a vocabulary with which to reflect on their daily work. Of course, the rules are often banal, trivial, or arguably wrongheaded. Nevertheless, they can be helpful. They start us thinking and trying out new approaches in our classrooms or modifying old ones, elaborating on something we've been doing already, or stopping some habitual activity the ineffectiveness of which has been brought to our attention.

After reviewing numerous studies of efforts to train teachers to raise the academic achievements of their students, Rosenshine and Stevens (1986) concluded "that there are specific instructional procedures which teachers can be trained to follow and which can lead to increased achievement and student engagement in their classrooms" (p. 376). The context here is one in which there is much more confidence in the significance of a set of truth statements about effective teaching, and in our capacity to train teachers in their implementation, than there is in teachers' ability to incorporate a set of ideas about instruction into their broader educational background and ongoing work. Rosenshine and Stevens go on to set up what they call a general model of effective instruction. They offer a set of desired teacher behaviors: examining homework, adducing new information, encouraging student practice, checking comprehension, correcting, and reteaching (1986, p. 379).

The authors elaborate on each of these instructional functions. For example, in their discussion of clear presentations, they advise the teacher to model the skill or process when appropriate, to offer detailed and redundant explanations for difficult points, and to provide students with concrete and varied examples. They remind us to check for student understanding by asking the students questions to monitor their comprehension and by having them summarize the main points in their own words. We are then to reteach the parts of the lesson the students haven't understood. Of course we know all these things already, and perhaps we really don't need extensive studies to support such directions. But the sort of elaborate directions to teachers that Rosenshine and Stevens offer in their article could serve the same function as the checklist offered in the writing workshop. If teachers are not following certain steps, they ought, like writers, to ask themselves why not. They may have good reasons for departing from the approaches suggested. But it is precisely the ability to reflect intelligently on the techniques suggested, to adapt and alter them to circumstances, and to ignore them at other times that seems to contribute so much to the making of good writers and teachers.

If context is not everything here, it is clearly significant. In teacher education, we need, above all, to discard the exclusive and silly model in which we see researchers building up a knowledge base of truths about which teachers may be certain, and from which they may develop specific behaviors to be used in classrooms, in order to increase levels of student achievement. Instead, teaching, like writing, ought to be viewed as an uncertain enterprise whose practitioners dip into a technical knowledge base from a perspective fueled by a broad academic and experiential background.

TECHNICAL PROFICIENCY IN TEACHING AND WRITING

A frequent criticism of writers' workshops is that as thousands and thousands of young and not so young writers around the country attend them, they are producing a very high level of technical proficiency and a sameness of style but are not graduating people with the imagination, passion, and originality needed to become truly great writers. Imagination, passion, and originality are seen as qualities central to the writer's task and not producible in workshops. Similarly, it is argued that the most essential aspects of teaching are not reducible to a set of learned techniques.

Drawing the line between the "merely technical" and the "something other" in both writing and teaching is difficult. There is, however, an important distinction to be made between those teachers and writers whose habitual approach is to take a set of directions and mechanically apply them and those who take a reflective, critical, and experimental stance toward new ideas about their work.

The issues we usually dismiss in writing and teaching as merely technical have an odd way, when pursued, of opening out into something more than the technical. The ways in which teachers and writers pursue these issues is all-important. To say that some piece of technical advice is all well and good but skirts the periphery of the "real issues" ignores the fact that technical concerns may be both perfectly legitimate in themselves—that is, useful in carrying forward the teacher or the writer's work—and also ways of gaining entrance to larger questions, the significance of which would not have been seen had the technical issue not arisen.

Questions, for example, about the writer's point of view in a given work might be dismissed as merely technical unless they are pursued in a serious fashion. A growing consciousness of the variety of points of view that a writer may choose to work from in handling a story and the limitations and possibilities that each choice affords, derived from an analysis of what other writers are doing and from a conscious experimentation with one's own work, soon leads one into an area of thinking about writing in which the "merely technical" gives way to the "something other."

Specific directions to teachers may be merely applied, or they may be responded to in an imaginative and thoughtful fashion. When teachers are told to offer concrete examples or to check for student comprehension, they may apply such advice in ways that will open them up to questions of the nature of definition, of how children learn, or of what constitutes adequate understanding, to name only a few. Aren't there successful writers and teachers who establish formulas for themselves and follow them without deviation? The answer depends on what we mean by successful. In my writing class, one student complained to the instructor about time spent on anything but a "how-to" approach. A Wall Street man, he had been impressed by the large amounts of money some writers earned from their books, and he wanted to get down to the business of learning a formula he could follow to make a buck himself. The instructor was certainly aware of the commercial realities of publishing and often mentioned that we could learn a great deal from authors we might dismiss as not so serious artists, but his essential project in the class was to help people write serious fiction, and he showed little patience with demands for money-making formulas. The instructor was saying that writing had a normative quality to it, and that inquiring into the nature of writing was as much an ongoing part of the writer's task as learning how to create strong, believable characters.

Many teachers look for formulas not for venal purposes but to attain order in their classrooms or to help their students achieve adequate scores on standardized tests. Their technical proficiency cuts them off from the possibility of further growth as teachers. Their refusal to embrace the uncertainty of the teacher's role is the real problem. Many teachers are skeptical about the claims of educational researchers that they are developing truth statements about educational practices, statements that, when learned and applied, will result in improved student learning. That is the sort of educational shortcut for which many teachers are looking, but they usually react to the actual truth claims by pointing out either that they are not new or that for some reason they will not work. They are cynics visiting the astrologer.

There is, of course, a profound truth at the heart of the distinction between the technical and the "something other" in both writing and teaching: Beyond any attention to questions of point of view, or imagery, or character development, good writers must have a wide and deeply reflective experience of the world that itself can be deepened in the writing act. One cannot teach this perspective directly and explicitly; it is affected by one's education and by the continued effort to render one's experience meaningful — that is, educational. A similar point can be made about the education of teachers. Enthusiasm for subject matter, alertness to the differences among young people, an interest in all the myriad factors in a society that affect the way children learn, a willingness to examine subject matter and methods in terms of larger educational purposes — these are not technical accomplishments, not reducible to a set of teacher behaviors that can be easily stated and in which teachers can be trained. But they are related to the education of teachers, to the task of encouraging teachers to become more alive to their own experience and discover the connections and the meanings within it, to become, as Gary Fenstermacher (1986) has said, students of their own work (p. 48).

THE LONELY PROFESSION

After a few weeks of the first semester of my writing workshop, a few of the students began meeting before class. We talked with one another about all aspects of our writing, suggested books to read, and traded our efforts with one another, giving and receiving critical comments from week to week. We found people whose comments we could trust, and we found the confidence in ourselves to incorporate those comments into our thinking about our own writing. This extension of the workshop was a valuable part of the whole experience.

Dan Lortie (1975) and others have commented on the problem of the isolation of the teacher. I think it worthwhile to examine the question of isolation and teaching in comparison with the isolation of the writer. I am talking here not just about the writing of fiction but about any sort of writing for publication, including academic writing. Clearly the writer's task is a lonely one. As a writer, finally, I must sit down by myself and produce the work. But most writers, at some stage of their work, seek comment and editorial advice from those whose judgment they respect. They talk with others about writing problems and about the substantive issues on which their writing is focused. They are interested in what other writers are doing and see themselves as part of a larger historical community of writers and thinkers. Finally, of course, there is the actual writing act, in which all of that involvement with others is transmuted into an autonomous production.

I think the teacher's situation tends to be quite different. There are

teachers who systematically and regularly sit down with their colleagues to talk about their daily work, who develop teaching materials
together, argue over curriculum matters, exchange classroom visits, and
generally provide feedback and support for one another. Such groups
are models for significant change in the direction of teacher education,
and, wherever they exist, we ought to find ways to sustain them. Unfortunately, not all such conversations are fruitful. The discussion in the
teachers' lounge tends to be dominated by personal comments about
students and by complaints about one's classes and other aspects of
the institution. Teachers' discussions in college classrooms tend to be
unrelated to the realities of the school, or, worse, to descend to the
level of the teachers' lounge complaining. It is hard to find contexts in
which the discourse of teachers is shaped by the experiential realities of
the classroom, open to helpful ideas from whatever sources are available, and designed to feed back into the teacher's work.

Lortie (1975) diagnoses the problem as the absence of a technical
vocabulary shared by teachers. "Teaching is not like crafts and professions, whose members talk in a language specific to them and their
work. Thus the absence of a common technical vocabulary limits a
beginner's ability to 'tap into' a preexisting body of practical knowledge" (p. 73). Without such a framework, Lortie argues, "the neophyte
is less able to order the flux and color of daily events and can miss
crucial transactions which might otherwise be encoded in the categories
of a developed discourse. Each teacher must laboriously construct ways
of perceiving and interpreting what is significant. That is one of the
costs of a mutual isolation which attends the absence of a common
technical culture" (p. 73). I think Lortie has come very close to something here, but he has not got it quite right. He speaks of a common
technical language and a common technical culture that he sees as
missing in teaching. I think that teachers of various subjects at different
grade levels need to develop a language of discourse about their work,
and that the language will have many sources. But essentially it should
grow out of individual teachers' reflective efforts to understand their
own work and to alter it for the better. The vocabularies of the psychologists and sociologists, the philosophers and the curriculum theorists,
are all in the running for incorporation into such a discourse, but clearly
a language for teachers and a common culture for teachers will have to
grow organically within cooperative enterprises by teachers, supported
with institutional commitments. We do, indeed, need a language to
talk about our work, as writers do. But writers talk about their work in
a language drawn largely from their general education, from their
reflections on their experiences, and from the everyday problems of

making words on pages. A language for teachers will have to grow in similar soil.

There is an extraordinary ferment within teacher education today; serious questions are being raised about the kinds of research that ought to be conducted, about the kind of knowledge that is useful in the education of teachers, and, perhaps most importantly, about how that knowledge is to be appropriated by teachers. Something far more than a technical vocabulary is at stake here. One direction this ferment is taking is illustrated in an article by Janet Miller (1987) reporting her work in teaching a "Writing Across the Curriculum" course to a group of in-service teachers. Rather than beginning with a body of concepts and information, she starts from the premise that teachers are storytellers. "Every teacher has a version of the drama, terror, and history of life in the classroom, and for a brief time that collective life seems a bit more manageable through the re-creation and sharing of these ongoing and often embellished sagas" (p. 193). Thus, rather than attempting to create a common culture through the introduction of a common technical vocabulary that the teachers might find useful, she begins with their own language and their own efforts to make meanings out of their lives inside and outside the classroom, "involving them not only in their own self-reflective research but also in classroom research" (p. 194). She emphasizes the active and collaborative roles of the teachers in this work. The vehicle for the reflective process was the writing of the teachers, some of whom reported that this was the first time they had ever written reflectively about their work. They were reading and writing the texts of their lives in classrooms and, perhaps more importantly, sharing them with others.

It seems to me that the case for modeling learning to teach on learning to write rather than on learning to be an engineer or a doctor rests, finally, on the fact that the most fundamental activities in which good teachers take part are more like the activities of writers than those of engineers or doctors. The teacher, like the writer, cannot arrive on the scene with a set of scientific laws to be applied to particular cases; the teacher, like the writer, must explore, interpret, and contribute to the construction of a complex and particular reality. Good writers usually do not impose a single set of meanings on their readers; they allow room for the reader to enter into the meaning-making process. So, too, good teachers take care to adopt a style and language that do not, as in the behavioral paradigm, seek to cause particular learning effects in students, but that invite them into the business of reflecting, imagining, and actively constructing their own worlds.

Learning to write played an important part in my education long before I enrolled in a writing workshop. I have always connected writing to thinking. This connection is not idiosyncratic. Rhetoric, the art of speaking and writing, has been at the heart of the liberal arts tradition. And liberal education has always defended itself on the grounds that it teaches students to think, to be actively engaged—most often through writing—in their own education. I will turn now to an inquiry into the place of teacher education in the larger context of this liberal education.

3

THE LIBERAL ARTS AND
LEARNING TO TEACH

The enlargement consists, not merely in the passive reception into the mind of a number of ideas hitherto unknown to it, but in the mind's energetic and simultaneous action upon and towards and among those new ideas, which are rushing in upon it. It is the action of a formative power, reducing to order and meaning the matter of our acquirements; it is a making the objects of our knowledge subjectively our own, or to use a familiar word, it is the digestion of what we receive, into the substance of our previous thought . . .
—*John Henry Newman (1976, p. 120)*

I have been contending that a teacher's education, even that part of it which we ordinarily call professional, ought not to be only technical. Some have argued that little remains to be done in the way of educating teachers after they have received a liberal education. Almost all the teacher education reformers active in the 1980s agree that teachers should have a strong liberal arts background. In some cases, it has been argued that those preparing to teach ought to major in a liberal arts subject and demonstrate an in depth understanding of it, as well as complete a distribution requirement in other liberal arts subjects. The argument is prompted by impatience with the quality of professional education courses and has led some undergraduate teacher education programs to require students to major in a liberal arts subject and take fewer education courses. Some institutions have dropped all or almost all undergraduate work in teacher education and moved it to the graduate level.

These curriculum debates, in focusing on course credit allotments and on the level at which courses are offered, have diverted attention from more important questions. Do liberal arts subjects prepare students to teach any more than they prepare students to work in other professions? What are the supposed educational purposes of study of the liberal arts? Does their fulfilment depend on the nature of the various subjects taught, on the ways in which they are taught, or on some combination of the two? These are the questions we should be asking about the liberal arts in relation to teacher education.

A few months before I began my college studies, I bought a Modern Library collection of Plato's dialogues. I found the questions and the arguments in those dialogues engaging. What is piety? What is virtue? What is the difference between knowledge and opinion? In one dialogue, Socrates would try to convince the court that it should find him innocent and not take his life, and in the next he would try to convince his friends that he must accept the verdict of the court and go to his death rather than escape from his cell. When I began traveling on the subway to St. Francis College, I had no specific career choice in mind, but I did want to join Socrates in pursuing these issues. (Professional sociologists and my own adult children have assured me that such is not the motive of typical college students in pursuing their education.)

In one course I took, we read some of the Greek tragedies. I sympathized with Antigone's willingness to flout Creon's interdict and bury her brother. For me the play raised a variety of questions about the relationships between the laws of the state and divine law, between individual freedom and authority, between doing what is right and saving one's own skin. The philosophical issues and concrete moral dilemmas I found in the writings of Sophocles, Plato, and others struck me as very real. My own reading was less a task to be accomplished for the accumulation of course credit than a way of deepening my experience of the world and defining new ways of living in it.

The way I experienced the world was dramatically altered by my college education. I was introduced to a particular style of inquiry, to a sense of the world's complexity, and to the myriad conceptual lenses through which we could view that complex world. I started to become aware of the tentative character of our very partial explanations and understandings of reality, and of the active role we students played in the achievement of these understandings. I began to see, too, the pervasiveness of the moral dimension in our lives, the flawed nature of a variety of historical visions of a just society, and the continuing human responsibility, nevertheless, to work to create a better world. I learned, in reading Socrates, the hard lesson that it is more important to pursue the truth than to win the argument, and that honest inquiry makes more sense than unreflective advocacy. My liberal education took me out of myself and the narrow world in which I lived. It introduced me to ways of thinking and being that I would not otherwise

have known. It has served me well as both a person and a teacher, and
so I am pleased that recent calls for the reform of teacher education
have included an insistence on the strengthening of the prospective
teacher's liberal arts preparation.

THE CURRENT SITUATION IN LIBERAL EDUCATION

We can better understand the place and value of a liberal education within a teacher's education if we look at some of the historical
and present arguments about what constitutes a liberal education and
examine the adequacy of the distinctions commonly offered among such
terms as *liberal, specialized,* and *professional.* Arguments over what
subjects are to be included in a liberal education are important; what
really makes a subject liberal, however, are the ways in which it is
taught and learned. From the students' point of view, the issue is how
subject matter is appropriated, how it is made a part of one's life and
work. I want to argue also that a better understanding of what it is to
be educated liberally leads us to see the remarkably complementary
relationship between such an education and the work of the teacher.

Curricular Relativism

It must seem odd, if nevertheless fortuitous, to the proponents of
liberal or general education that reformers in teacher education should
look to it for help at a time when it is in such disarray. Supporters of
liberal education have been convinced for some time that they are
fighting a losing battle. Contemporary theories of knowledge challenge
the very notion of a defined body of truth. That the colleges do not
offer a unified set of courses to their undergraduates is not, however, so
much a failure of intellectual nerve on the part of the professors, as
William Bennett tells us (1986, p. 20), as it is a recognition of the
complexity of the way in which we come to know the world.

The dream of a hierarchically organized, unified curriculum that
all should follow is no longer a viable one. The relativist insight that
values claimed to be rooted in divine or natural law are, in fact, the
product of particular historical circumstances; the recognition by the
sociologists of knowledge that our ideas, values, and institutions are not
objective givens but shared human inventions—these and a host of
other insights all conspire against the possibility of a single, unified
curriculum. Impressed by the evanescence of things and values, we
have become tentative about what we should pass on to our children.

It is not that since the nineteenth century things have been falling apart and the center not holding. This has always been the situation. It is just that we have had the good sense to take note of it. We recognize that there is no single, coherent, historical narrative and no univocal set of values to hand to young people. To assert otherwise — to extract a large-scale systemic meaningfulness from the confusion that surrounds us — is to engage in an indefensible nostalgia. The difficulty of our cultural situation, as we shall see, need not result in a curricular nihilism. There are still better and worse ways to learn.

Career Orientation

Aside from this larger cultural context, which raises questions about the traditional content of a liberal education, the particular social context in which American colleges operate seems to negate the stated purposes of a liberal arts education. A student once told me that the reason he wanted a liberal arts diploma was so that he might have an edge in the business world over his friends, who were majoring in accounting or computer science. He would be able to write well and they wouldn't. He reflects, in a display of unintended irony, the pervasive concern with social and economic mobility that the sociologists tell us is the real engine of the American system of higher education. This is nothing new. Lawrence Vesey (1965) assures us that at the turn of the century the student who said, "The degree from Harvard College is worth money to me in Chicago" (p. 270), nicely reflected the temper of those times. The liberal arts colleges continue to sell their general education to prospective students and their parents on the same grounds, just as business leaders continue to affirm the value of a liberal education.

The once haughty liberal arts have been forced by circumstance to embrace the very institutions and values from which they previously took pains to distinguish themselves. It is an uneasy coupling. What is our student, wishing to get an edge on his fellow students, to think when he comes to read Socrates' admonition to the court that has just condemned him to death? "Punish my sons, gentlemen, if you think they care for money or for anything else before virtue."

For years, proponents of the liberal arts fought against the inclusion of any vocationally oriented course or program in the undergraduate college curriculum. The content of most college catalogues would seem to indicate, nevertheless, that the spirit of vocationalism has come to dominate college campuses. Given that colleges operate within the context of a pervasive concern with social mobility, it would be wise to reexamine the traditional stated purposes of the liberal arts and the manner in which these purposes relate to the experience of contemporary college students. I am especially concerned here with the question of whether a conflict exists between the stated purposes of a liberal education and the purposes of those preparing for a career in teaching.

Specialization and Professionalization

Vocationalism has been accompanied by the related phenomenon of specialization. Neither specialization nor professionalization is necessarily antithetical to the purposes of the liberal arts. Historically, however, both have had a pernicious effect on those purposes. Once President Eliot of Harvard and others succeeded in establishing the principle that a variety of subject areas could be liberalizing, colleges moved toward departmentalization, and the system of majors emerged. The subsequent history of American colleges has been marked by an increase in the power of departments, in the influence of the graduate and professional schools on the undergraduate curriculum, and, of course, in specialization within the undergraduate college.

The major has taken up more and more of the undergraduate curriculum, while the general course of study has become a set either of distribution requirements or of mandated survey courses. Nor have the various college departments taken great care to design the courses fulfilling the distribution requirements so that they reflect the purposes of a liberal education. Faculty seem more interested in preparing students for specialized work than in exploring the relevance of their discipline to the students' general educations.

At this moment in the history of general or liberal arts education, the reformers of teacher education have chosen to look to it for salvation. What are the implications, for teachers pursuing a general education, of the situation in which the liberal arts finds itself? Given the impossibility of a unified curriculum reflecting a set of agreed-upon truths and values, given the context of money and career concerns in which general education is carried out, given the growth of specialization and its tendency to diminish energies devoted to a more general education, how are teachers to go about the task of acquiring a genuinely liberal education?

HOW WE TEACH AND LEARN

Theorists of liberal education have recognized for some time the fruitlessness of the search for a unified curriculum, for an acceptable content that might be defined as the essence of a liberal education. They have been inquiring, instead, into the sorts of teaching and learning approaches to knowledge that will be most liberating for students, that are most likely to attain the traditional goals of a liberal education. Students enrolling in a liberal arts or general education sequence today should recognize that they will acquire no single history of the world, no canon of great literature and art, and no set of unquestioned human values. Instead, they will face a curriculum that recognizes plural understandings of the past and acknowledges the extent to which all of these understandings are themselves human inventions, both enlarged and limited by a particular set of historical concerns. Wise students will begin to perceive the very human process through which we have gone about constructing sets of standards for our great literature and art. They will recognize that the concepts of the various disciplines do not mirror the world but rather allow us to understand it in ways that we might otherwise have not. At the same time, they may cut us off from other ways of understanding. The modern novelist seeks to remind readers that they are not reading about the real world, but inhabiting a work of fiction; the modern artist shocks the viewer into a recognition of the artifice involved in the work of art. The student, it seems to me, must adopt this perspective, must treat text and curriculum not as reflections of the world but as both helpful and limiting constructions of reality.

Recognizing that there is no single coherent story to tell about the world, no canon of great literature and art, no accepted set of values to be passed along to the next generation, many twentieth-century statements of the purposes of a liberal arts education, descriptions of curricula, and principles for the organization of a curriculum express a concern with the *manner* in which material is presented and learned, rather than trying to choose exactly the right material. Thus, Philip Phenix (1964) tells us that "It is more important for the student to become skilful in the ways of knowing than to learn about any particular product of investigation. Knowledge of methods makes it possible for a person to continue learning and to undertake inquiries on his own. Furthermore, the modes of thought are far less transient than are the products of inquiry" (p. 11). We have given up learning the eternal verities in exchange for learning effective ways to go about learning. The crucial issue becomes how one goes about learning any subject in a way that will increase its liberating potential.

Jerome Bruner (1960) talks about giving students an understanding of the fundamental structure of the subjects learned. Again, the purpose is to prepare the student for further learning. "If earlier learning is to render later learning easier, it must do so by providing a general picture in terms of which the relations between things encountered earlier and later are made as clear as possible" (p. 12). In Daniel Bell's (1966) important work on general education, we also find this insistence that the liberalizing aspect of a subject is not a function of its content as much as of the manner of its presentation.

> When a subject is presented as received doctrine or fact, it becomes an aspect of specialization or technique. When it is introduced with an awareness of its contingency, and of the conceptual frame that guides its organization, the student can then proceed with the necessary self-consciousness that keeps his mind open to possibility and reorientation. All knowledge, thus, is liberal (that is, it enlarges and liberates the mind) when it is committed to continuing inquiry. (p. 8)

PREPARATION FOR TEACHING:
THE LIBERAL IS THE USEFUL

The two other difficulties in which liberal arts education finds itself today are closely related to each other. The dominant meaning assigned to a college education in our society is that it is a path to a career; consequently, the undergraduate curriculum in most colleges tends to be specialized and concerned with preparing students for graduate and professional study and for the world of business. The liberal arts tradition has alternated between remaining aloof from this vocationalization of the colleges, and, more recently, embracing it unthinkingly. Teachers should be especially interested in this question of the relationship between professional preparation and a more general education. I said at the outset of this chapter that when I began my undergraduate work, I was not at all certain about my choice of a career and hence did not see my studies from a utilitarian point of view. I was fascinated by a set of questions about the meaning of my life in the world, and I was optimistic that inquiries into philosophy, psychology, literature, and history would help me to better understand these issues and to act in the world. The fact that a student is interested in something for other than utilitarian motives does not render what is learned useless. One may be fascinated by how people go about building bridges; such fascination may well lead to learning that proves useful later on. We simply do not know where our early interests will lead us.

An impatient utilitarianism that seeks to know how each topic or idea discovered in a general education curriculum relates to one's career cuts the learner off from the possibility of genuine growth. Learners are fascinated by all sorts of things: by large explanatory schemes such as Darwin's notion of natural selection working on chance variations of organisms; by the pursuit of questions such as "What is friendship?"; or by an account of an archeological discovery, or the careful analysis of a poem, or the presentation of a geometrical theorem. Fascination with these and hundreds of other ideas is at the heart of a liberal education.

Need we ask whether such interests are useful to teachers? Deliver the schools from those who are strangers to such excitement! When we teach, we often find useful things that we have been drawn to and fascinated by, and hence learned, with no external application in mind. They are useful because our students sense our interest and fascination and want to be in on the action. They are useful because such interests lead to a mastery of subjects and enable teachers not only to inspire interest but to guide students through sustained and comprehensive inquiry. For teachers as learners, the distinction between liberal and useful learning simply does not hold. What is learned in a liberal fashion turns out to be the most useful in the work of the teacher.

In order to understand the ambiguous reaction of defenders of the liberal tradition in education to purposes such as individual and social utility, it is important to grasp the larger world view within which the liberal arts tradition has developed. This view is rooted in the mind/body dualism that has had such deleterious effects on western culture. Leisure was seen as the great good of man and a necessary condition for the exercise of freedom. Work and activity were associated with strain and tension. Unhurried contemplation was preferred to observation and experimentation. The development and study of theories and principles was seen as an appropriate activity for the gentleman; the making and doing of things according to plan was the task of the functionary (Pieper, 1952).

Many defenders of the liberal arts in our own century have operated from within this tradition. They espouse an academic purity and are not interested in helping the farmers look after the cows or preparing people for specific vocations. Robert Maynard Hutchins (1936) and others believed that a study of the liberal arts cultivated the intellectual virtues and that these virtues were good in themselves. Thus, he could write, "All that can be learned in a university is the general principles, the fundamental propositions, the theory of any discipline" (p. 48).

Hutchins worked from an understanding of knowledge embedded in the dualistic world view described above. The sometimes useful distinction between intellectual and practical activity is here treated as if there were no significant connection between the two spheres. My own sense of the matter is that principles, fundamental propositions, and theories are best understood within contexts of application, that they do not exist in a Platonic realm outside of this world but rather become part of what we mean by a sophisticated experiencing of this world. Hutchins insisted that even professional schools should avoid "vocationalism" and focus on principles and theory. The university's task, he believed, was the intellectual training of the young, teaching them how to reason so that they would be able to assimilate and comprehend their future experiences. Here again, Hutchins was working from the conceptual split between reason and experience that has had such a disastrous effect on our educational thinking and practice.

He derided the curriculum of the divinity schools, where, according to him, prospective clergy learned about "building management and community and church socials and what is called religious education" (p. 46). His derisory tone emanated from the world view and the consequent theory of knowledge that Hutchins embraced. His clergy would study only the principles of theology. But of course one must seek the connections between theology and the daily activities of the clergy so that the theology will be a directing force in the clergy's daily activity and that the activities themselves can be a challenge to the stated theology.

Hutchins took the same attitude toward the education of teachers as he took toward the education of the clergy. "All there is to journalism," Hutchins tells us, "can be learned through a good education and newspaper work. All there is to being a teacher can be learned through a good education and being a teacher" (1936, p. 56). When Hutchins refers here to a good education, he, of course, means a liberal education of the sort that aggressively separates theory from practice, leisure from the work of the world.

John Dewey spent a good part of his professional career trying to overcome the set of dichotomies to which Hutchins and many others subscribed. Teachers rethinking the nature of their own liberal education and its relation to their professional preparation would do well to recall Dewey's (1950) insight, "A philosophic reconstruction which should relieve men of having to choose between an impoverished and truncated experience, on the one hand, and an artificial and impotent reason on the other, would relieve human effort from the heaviest intellectual burden it has to carry" (p. 92). Hutchins and others have defined and defended a liberal arts education as precisely the sort of artificial and impotent vehicle of which Dewey speaks in his characterization of the way in which human reason has historically been construed. For

Hutchins, a liberal education shuns utility wherever it makes a claim; it is to take place on the university campus, separate from the workaday world. It emphasizes reason and first principles, which are conceived as existing outside of and prior to the world of human experience. It focuses only on a set of texts and not on the world from which the texts ultimately derive. Note that Dewey's reconstruction is equally concerned with eliminating "an impoverished and truncated experience," a description that might nicely be applied to certain "practical" education courses and to some kinds of teaching experience undergone in isolation from the spirit of a liberal education.

Teachers must work at the task of integrating the liberal and professional components in teacher education. When we have acquired an education appropriate for us as human beings, we shall have gone a long way toward acquiring an education for ourselves as teachers. It is appropriate to view the specialized or professional segment of a teacher's education not simply as an opportunity to develop a set of competencies separate from those needed to become more fully human but as an intensification and application of the humanistic qualities to a specific area of our lives. There surely is a sense in which our own education has no other purpose beyond itself, that is, no other purpose than to produce in us the capacity for further growth. There remains, however, the question of the next generation; the teacher's role is to see that the capacity for growth takes on a social and historical reality, that it does not end with the teacher as student.

There is a reciprocal relationship in this business of learning so that we may teach. Teachers with whom I have had extended conversations about teaching point out that they have only learned something well when they have had to teach it. The project of teaching a novel, or developing a scientific explanation for a set of phenomena, or showing students the connections among historical events, forces us to look anew at what is to be taught. We teach so that we may learn. The effort to isolate what is instrumental and what an end product in the general education of teachers is fruitless.

A liberal education, well begun, should prepare teachers to be more reflective about the issues with which they are faced daily. When I taught English at the secondary level during the late 1950s and early 1960s, some of us began to raise questions about the issues of race and inequality at home and about our involvement in Southeast Asia abroad. Such issues inevitably entered my classroom discussions as we read writers as diverse as Thoreau and Kipling, Wilfrid Owen and Carl Sandburg. I also asked myself: What was my role as a teacher handling such significant moral issues in a classroom? Was I to remain neutral? Was I to be objective? Was it possible to argue moral issues in the same way that one argued "factual" issues? I think that the style of thinking and the set of concerns that had interested me since my first reading of Socrates' questions stood me in good stead here. The issues of my daily life as a teacher became matters of serious reflection for me, and the manner in which I carried out my teaching tasks was influenced by these reflections. This was clearly not a case of learning specific teaching methods or using some piece of acquired knowledge; it was a case of extending and applying a habit of inquiry to some very real issues in my life as a teacher. It is, of course, precisely the inculcation of such habits of reflection that the proponents of a liberal arts education claim as their most important goal.

In a school district in which I taught during the early 1960s, the high school students were divided into four tracks: an honors class and A, B, and C tracks. For those of us teaching at all of these levels simultaneously, it was hard not to notice that the students in the honors class tended to come from a different part of town than the students in the C track. Differences in ethnicity were also related to differences in class assignments. I still recall a young man in my first-period honors class observing a student from a later C-track class of mine waving to me on his way to an auto-shop class down the hall. The honors student's reaction was to ask me, "Mr. Proefriedt, how do you know people like that?" Apparently this young man was not aware of the then widely accepted notion that the comprehensive high school was doing away with class distinctions in our society. Since my early years in teaching I have been interested in the complex relationship between the economic realities of our society and school practices.

Certain courses in a general education sequence, albeit not designed with an eye to possible application by teachers in their classrooms, may nevertheless provide a conceptual framework useful in addressing the everyday problems of classrooms. Consider a young teacher in an urban setting who is faced with a roomful of students of varied linguistic and cultural backgrounds. How does she experience the class? The answer depends a great deal, of course, on what she brings to the experience. Some new teachers bring to their work only the prejudices of the segment of the society of which they are a part, joining these to attitudes already existing in the school setting. If new teachers bring to such an experience no sociolinguistic sophistication, then their experience is likely to be, in Dewey's words, "impoverished and truncated"— impoverished by the narrowness of their own perspective. On the other hand, a teacher who has been exposed to the scientific approach and the conceptual apparatus offered in a course in sociolinguistics might have a quite different experience in her classroom. She would bring to it some understanding of the connections between language and personal identity, language and group solidarity, and language and social mobility. One cannot, of course, guarantee that a study of sociolinguistics will significantly alter the way in which young teachers experience cultural and linguistic differences in their classrooms. But teachers can set themselves the task of studying a significant issue, language in its social context; they can equip themselves with a developed conceptual structure, sociolinguistics, to aid in the inquiry; and, in all of this, they seem to be taking a reasonable gamble that their educational effort will be both liberating (in a traditional sense) and useful. At the same time, schools and classrooms can provide teacher-researchers with a rich and vital context for inquiry into sociolinguistic issues and for efforts to work out the educational implications of the understandings acquired.

Teachers have only to abandon an outdated theory of knowledge that insists on a split between reason and experience, between thought and action, between the pursuit of truth and service to the community, in order to construct for themselves a genuinely liberal education. This construction can take place in courses labeled liberal or professional, and in school settings labeled "experience." Some of the most articulate defenders of the liberal arts tradition have seen the need to overcome these dichotomies in our thinking about education. Thus, Jacques Maritain (1943), in a passage outlining the directions in which a renewed humanistic education should move, writes, "And the education of tomorrow must bring to an end, too, the cleavage between work or useful activity and the blossoming of spiritual life and disinterested joy in knowledge and beauty" (p. 89). Josef Pieper (1952), another thoughtful defender of the liberal arts tradition, speaks with sympathy of the "attempt to extend the character of 'liberal art' deep down into every human action, even the humblest servile work" (p. 69). The comments of each of these thinkers, it seems to me, point in the direction of a transformed education and experience for teachers — transformed by the recognition that we need not stay imprisoned in outworn cultural and conceptual structures. What follows from an effort to overthrow the standard argument over liberal versus technical education is, clearly, not only a change in the ways in which institutions, faculty, and students approach liberal arts courses, but also a change in the way in which we conceive the professional dimensions of teacher education and a change in the direction of making that education a more liberal and less technical experience (Borrowman, 1956). Much of the rest of this book addresses the question of how we ought to liberalize the professional dimension of a teacher's education.

In the next chapter, I will describe how I have used Plato's *Republic* in a philosophy of education course. Plato's work is, of course, a staple in a traditional liberal education. At the same time, it is a useful text in the professional education of teachers.

4

USING A PHILOSOPHICAL TEXT IN THE EDUCATION OF TEACHERS

A too-narrow definition of what is useful for teachers to learn pervades many teacher preparation programs. Traditional academic inquiries into significant texts are sacrificed to courses with titles such as "Classroom Management" that promise specific prescriptions for teachers with immediate problems to handle. Teacher educators often respond unreflectively to demands for practicality from students and school people. To some, philosophy — for example, the work of Plato — does not lead the list of topics useful for teachers. Most teacher educators, in a reversal of the academic ethos, view teaching a course in the philosophy of education as a less serious enterprise than running a field-based program or teaching a "practical" course (such as "Classroom Management"). There is, nevertheless, some disagreement over just what sort of course content is practical.

There are a number of interconnected reasons why teacher educators dismiss the study of classical texts. The first reason is a general cultural one, of which I spoke in my first chapter. We Americans are celebrated or condemned as practical-minded folk, anti-ideological in our politics, engineers rather than pure theoreticians. Hence, we don't want to be caught idly contemplating a classical text with a group of young teachers, when we might better be spending our time showing them how to engineer classroom behavior. The second one is the general vocational tilt in American colleges, to which I referred in Chapter 3. Students choose practical courses and majors such as accounting and computer science, and traditional general education subjects earn their keep only insofar as they demonstrate their usefulness in preparing students for the workplace. The relevance of Plato to the work of the classroom teacher is not immediately apparent. A third reason for the avoidance of classical texts is more immediate. New teachers often find themselves in difficult teaching situations and seek help in the form of specific instructions for handling their classes. Teacher educators try to respond to these requests and thereby lose confidence in those aspects of their program which seek to develop larger perspectives in their students. Finally, an important approach in teacher education, as we have seen, has conceived of it in very "practical" terms as the identification of those teacher behaviors that lead to increased learning in students and the training of teachers in these behaviors.

Philosophy was held in ill-repute in Plato's day also, a disfavor which he accounted for in two ways. First, many clever people who were not serious lovers of truth went about putting on airs and pretending to be philosophers, and thereby made themselves obnoxious. Secondly, the real philosophers tended to point out to other citizens that they were disputing about unrealities, whereupon the citizens, convinced of the importance of their own arguments, dismissed the philosophers as stargazers.

Plato saw the ability to turn individuals away from one set of interests toward another as the essence of education. Education, for him, was not a matter of instilling intelligence in individuals, but of turning that intelligence in the right direction. "Have you never noticed in men who are said to be wicked but clever, how sharply their little soul looks into things to which it turns its attention?" (519a)

I do not see the world of teacher education as being quite so dichotomous as Plato's world, but I think it fair to say that the dismissal of a philosophical approach in the education of teachers stems from a focus on what many consider to be important — but what in fact turns out to be shadows and images on the walls of the cave. In our anxiety to be responsive to the problems of teachers and schools, we have accepted the narrowest definitions of those problems and encouraged the teachers to do the same. In the process, we have forgotten the need to question current definitions of the problems and to lead teachers to question them as well.

PLATO'S PROJECT AND OURS

One way among the many in which teachers can be encouraged to reflect on their work is through the spirited analysis of important philosophical texts that focus on educational issues. Plato's *Republic* is, of course, one such text. Over the years many individuals have tried to develop ways of "applying" philosophy to education, but it seems to me that since philosophers have directly addressed educational problems, the main task of teacher educators is to help teachers understand and engage intellectually with these philosophers' texts. Trust teachers to bring their own experience to bear on the text, and trust the text to provide them with some distance and perspective on their everyday problems and to alter the ways in which they experience their work.

I am, of course, not suggesting that teachers should read Plato because of the set of doctrines he offers about education and society. What is most important is that teachers understand the project in which Plato is engaged and that they emulate him in their own speech and writing about his work and theirs; that they, in Newman's words, "make the objects of our knowledge subjectively our own" (1976, p. 120). What teacher educators can do in teaching the *Republic* is to call to the attention of teachers certain aspects of the project in which Plato is engaged, and to invite them to consider those aspects for incorporation into their own work as teachers.

The Connectedness of Things

During my first few years of teaching, I was disturbed by the way in which so many things in the classroom were intricately connected with one another. If students were doing poorly, there was often some emotional upset interfering with their learning. A gifted class was almost invariably composed of students from upper-middle-class homes; individuals in lower-track classes were frequently from poorer homes. Students' motivation and achievement were clearly tied to broader patterns in their lives. What sorts of things was I as a teacher to take into consideration when deciding what to do about a student's disruptive behavior in my classroom, or about a student's grades or placement? The connections I saw were disturbing because they revealed the complexity of situations about which I and other teachers and school administrators had to make decisions. There was always a need to take in more information, to understand the various connections more clearly, followed, often, by a realization that the available options were all unsatisfactory. Attempts to decide what was best for an individual student, then, often led to critiques of existing school practices and purposes and, finally, to questions about the larger society and the school's relation to it.

This effort to understand the complexity of school problems sometimes leads to a bitterness in serious teachers who see the causes of the problems they face daily as being outside their control. Whatever decisions they make about class discipline, grading, or guidance seem inadequate. Hence the railing against the system whose mechanisms remain undefined, and the frustration with one's own role as an ineffectual actor in the school play. Too many teachers withdraw from the enormously difficult task of continuing to examine the larger context and acting thoughtfully, and in concert with others, within it; they find the life project of the teacher too difficult to pursue.

Enter philosophy and Plato. It is characteristic of Plato and of philosophers in general to try to see things in their larger contexts. In reading the *Republic*, one becomes aware that Plato is struggling to see and to articulate the connections among all things. He is aware of the problems this causes him. At the end of Book 1, for example, he has Socrates bemoaning the fact that he seems to be jumping from one subject to another, "as gluttons do, snatching at every dish that passes them, and tasting it before they have reasonably enjoyed the one before" (354b). It is disturbing, at first, in reading the *Republic*, to see Plato jump about, first telling us about the characteristics of the philosopher, then stating the differences between knowledge and opinion, then distinguishing between the phenomenal and the real world (473–480). But it is precisely this effort to see things in relation to one another, to develop a synoptic view, that, for Plato, characterizes the education of the philosopher (536c). The synoptic view taken in the *Republic* challenges teachers not to turn away in bitterness from the task of examining the experiences they have in their own classrooms in larger and larger contexts, but instead to recognize that they are part of a tradition of teachers and thinkers who have reflected seriously on the educative calling as they have pursued it. Plato, too, was disturbed by the question of what one did with understandings of situations that did not seem to be useful within "the system." There are moments in the *Republic* when he, too, seems to despair of the possibility that people with a philosophical nature can play any practical role in the city (496c).

In the *Republic*, all is connected. Plato begins with the questions of what justice is and whether it is better to be just or unjust. He points up the shortcomings of different views of justice, and, in order to find out what it really is and whether it is worth pursuing, he looks for it on a larger canvas than that of the individual; he describes how a city comes to be and how it functions. He sees justice not as existing in some particular group in the city but as each person acting in accordance with his natural role and not interfering with the work of others. Justice in the individual soul is a matter of each of the parts of the soul attending to its own business.

Plato describes both the city and the soul as divided into three parts. The rational part, because it has wisdom, or real knowledge of the way things are, is suited for the task of determining how the city or the individual should go about life. The spirited part, seeking glory, enhances the individual and the city and protects against harm. The

pleasure-seeking or money-making part, in a well-ordered state or individual, will be subordinated to the part of the society or soul that is
rational and wise and, therefore, knows which pleasures to seek and
which to avoid in order to serve the long-term interest of the individual
and the society.

How are we to produce such a well-ordered (that is, just) individual and state? For Plato, the chief instrument for the task is education —
more specifically, a certain type of education determined by the nature
of the task. The purpose and practice of education is determined by an
understanding of what constitutes the good individual and the good
society. One cannot talk seriously about educational issues without understanding their connections to these questions: What sorts of individuals are just? What sorts of societies are just? Is it worthwhile for both
the individual and the society to pursue justice?

As if understanding these connections were not a difficult enough
task, Plato adds other elements for our consideration. In order to plan
our educational practice, we need also to know something about the
nature of knowledge and the nature of the reality we have knowledge
about. The answers to the more frequently asked questions — "What is
to be taught? How is it to be taught? To whom shall it be taught?" —
have then to be rooted not only in a psychology and a social theory,
which are at once normative and descriptive, but also in an understanding of the nature of knowledge and of the world that knowledge knows.

My summary does a disservice to the intertwining tendrils in Plato's
teeming forest. There are in the *Republic* a richness of psychological
description, a sense of the realities of political life, and a capacity for a
metaphorical rendering of the situations in which we find ourselves
that are brought to bear in the effort to answer interlocking questions
about individuals, education, and society. Plato is aware of the enor-
mity of his task, but he has not turned away from it. He offers us a
model of tenacious philosophical inquiry and does not allow the connectedness of things, and the need to translate our understanding of
the connectedness into practical activity, to drive him to despair. Nor
should we.

Sustained Analysis and Moral Seriousness

Plato searches for a definition of justice. He is dissatisfied with both
the traditional answer (which Polemarchus attributes to Simonides), that
justice is doing good to one's friends and harm to one's enemies (332),
and with the "modern" notion of Thrasymachus, that justice is the
making of laws to their own advantage by those in power (338c–339).

He questions Polemarchus and Thrasymachus in an effort to clarify their positions and to examine the implications of their claims. It turns out that many of us, like Polemarchus and Thrasymachus, have not quite clarified in our own thinking various ideas that we assume or espouse, and that we are not always willing to accept the implications of the positions we take when these implications are pointed out to us. Socrates questions both the accepted belief and the shocking modern opinion. It is not the questioning alone that is significant. As Socrates knew, any wise guy can do that. What is important is the sustained intellectual inquiry that follows upon the questioning. This careful examination of concepts we use is another aspect of Plato's project, another dimension of any serious philosophical project, that teachers might be encouraged to incorporate into their own work.

The inquiry is not just an academic exercise, but a truly serious business. "Or do you think it is a small thing to decide on a whole way of living which, if each of us adopted it, would make him lead the most profitable life?" (344e) Glaucon and Adeimantus are really troubled by reports that men make laws only to avoid being harmed by others — that if they could practice injustice themselves, and not be harmed by others in turn, they would do it. The making of laws, in this view, is a compromise that would not be made by men who had the power to do as they pleased and to defend themselves against others (359). Glaucon and Adeimantus find these reports persuasive, and yet they continue to believe that it is, nevertheless, worthwhile to lead a just life. They want Socrates to provide a rational basis for their belief so that they may go on maintaining it, and they wish to hear a defense of justice that shows it to be worthwhile in itself, not just for the rewards and honors received by those who appear to be just. Intellectual inquiry is here entwined with a moral quest. The tone is one of high seriousness, as it should be when one is engaged in the enterprise of teaching and learning about how to live one's life.

Going Where the Argument Takes Us

Over and over in the *Republic*, Plato insists that we should go where the argument takes us. He does not, in order to gain disciples, avoid providing us with reasons that challenge his position. He invites his listeners and readers to offer counterarguments, and he even pauses at one point to point out his own fears in presenting certain beliefs about which he is very much in doubt. "I fear that I may not only lose my own footing in my search for the truth, but also drag down my friends in my fall where a false step should least occur" (451b). Plato invites us to challenge him, and he is often eminently challengeable. If teachers are to take him as a model, they will need first to study and understand his argument, then to see its implications, and, finally, to offer alternative directions of their own.

Plato's position on censorship offers teachers an opportunity to exercise their own skill at philosophical inquiry. Most teachers in America, as we move toward the twenty-first century, are against censorship. Most teacher educators want teachers to be against censorship and perhaps even to be able to offer a few reasons why. A teacher education worth its salt will be more concerned, however, with encouraging teachers to examine their beliefs than with defining the content of those beliefs. Reading Book 4 of the *Republic* cursorily, most teachers reaffirm their belief that censorship is unacceptable despite Plato's argument for it. What they believe at that point, however, is largely irrelevant pedagogically. The important first step for the teacher educator is to encourage the teachers to understand Plato's argument for censoring Homer and the other poets within the context of Plato's other concerns in the *Republic*.

Plato is interested in educating the guardians, whose tasks will include protecting everyone in the city against invasions from outside. The good of the whole city is paramount, and, in order for that good to be secured, the guardians must be able to carry out their role. Plato believes that if they are educated properly, the guardians will have little need for legislation to govern them, just as men who diet and exercise properly will have little need for medicine. But the education must be carefully thought out. On the negative side, nothing will be admitted into it which might dissuade the guardians from carrying out their assigned tasks; on the positive side, its content must be shaped to form the character of the guardians in ways suitable to the tasks assigned to them.

Plato asks, "Shall we then carelessly allow the children to hear any kind of stories composed by anybody, and to take into their souls beliefs which are for the most part contrary to those we think they should hold in maturity?" (377c) It is a powerful question. He wishes to expurgate from the tales of the poets all references to an underworld full of terrors, to the lamentations of famous men, to violent mood changes in gods and heroes, to all varieties of immoderate behavior. It is the shaping of the character of the guardians in the interest of the safety of the city that is at stake, and Plato is willing to throw out anything that might make them fearful of death or provide them with examples of undesirable behavior.

He will control the storytellers by selection and rejection of their

stories as appropriate for the education of the guardians, and by offering them general guidelines. The issue, for Plato, turns out to be not so
much merely censorship as a concern with shaping the character of the
individual and the city. He even suggests that, in the interests of the
city, all shall be told a noble lie: that their upbringing and education
was merely a dream and that they were really fashioned inside the
earth, some mixed with gold, some silver, and some bronze. They are
all brothers, but their separate roles must be preserved.

The effort to understand Plato's argument for censorship within
the structure of his assumptions and purposes inevitably leads teachers
to compare and contrast our own educational purposes and practices
with his. Teachers note, for example, that we, too, often shape our
histories and stories for moral and social purposes. We, too, have our
noble lies or myths that tend to justify the economic and political realities of our society. We seem, however, to have a quite different sense of
the role of individuals and the legitimacy of their claims within society.
The implications of each view for the ways that society makes educational decisions can be examined. Teachers can explore alternative ways
in which schools might develop a moral education within the context of
American cultural commitments to the importance of individual freedom. To go where the argument leads them, as Plato would have them
do, is, for teachers, inevitably, to explore the complexities of their own
situation.

The Focus on Educational Purpose

Another characteristic activity of Plato is to focus on purposes.
Educational purposes are rarely treated in a philosophical way in programs of teacher education. They may be viewed as too vague to have
much to do with the daily activities of the teacher. They may be impa-
tiently abandoned in favor of the training of teachers in the formulation
of behavioral outcomes. In the schools, too often, we see statements of
educational purpose tucked away in closets or distributed to parents in
the interest of public relations; in some classrooms, teachers write a
goal for their lesson on the blackboard whenever a supervisor is visiting
them, and sometimes even when they are alone with the children. Too
seldom, however, do teachers try to examine educational purposes with
the kind of seriousness that Plato brings to the question of how we shall
lead our lives.

And that is the question at stake whenever there is serious talk
about educational goals. In Books 8 and 9 of the *Republic*, in which

Plato describes the various types of corrupted cities and—in a bravura display of descriptive psychology—the character types that produce and are produced by these cities, he has Glaucon agree that in the oligarchic or money-loving city and man, "Possessions are certainly held in honour." The oligarchic man is not one who "pays any attention to education." He has chosen Plutus, the god of wealth, as "the blind leader of his dance" (554b). For Plato, not only was the achieving of wealth not a goal for education, but a man who set his sights on the achievement of wealth, over all other concerns, was considered to have no interest in education.

Recall that Plato's definition of education was tied to a view of the person and society in which each part stood in the proper relation to the other parts. In an individual, therefore, if the part of the soul that demanded honors, or the part that sought money, or the part that was ruled by competing pleasures, got the better of the rational part of the soul, then education, in Plato's terms, simply had not taken place. For the purpose of education was to produce harmony in the individual and in the city—a harmony in which the philosophical or rational part, the part that demonstrated wisdom by judging what was best for the individual and the city in the long run, remained in charge.

The notion of an education aimed at achieving fame or wealth was quite simply a contradiction for Plato. In our own day, some may find aspects of Plato's thinking about education narrow, shortsighted, or even offensive. His positions, however, are articulated so systematically in relation to a broader human psychology and social ethic that a close analysis of his whole argument leads teachers to a more serious look at the broader purposes of their own work. We begin to examine what and how we teach, and to look at the economic, racial, and cultural realities of our society. We begin to align our educational practice and purpose with our conception of what sort of lives we think individuals and societies ought to lead. We begin to make the same sorts of connections for our society that Plato made for his own. But unless we as teachers have wrestled with the sorts of questions that Plato invites us to consider, we will not internalize questions of educational purpose and seek to translate them into daily practice.

Plato's psychology of the soul and his educational philosophy are both tied to his conviction that there are better and worse ways to lead one's life, and to his belief that he has, indeed, found the better way. He has made his choice; of the three sorts of lives one can live—that of the lover of wisdom, the lover of victory and glory, or the lover of money—that of the lover of wisdom is best. A good part of the *Republic* is devoted to arguing the case for his choice. The content and practice of Plato's education is everywhere informed by his inquiry into what constitutes the good life. No lesser ideal should be embraced by teachers.

Challenging Student Opinions

The confrontational aspect of the Socratic pedagogy is justified by the moral conviction at the heart of the enterprise. The young person of philosophical temperament is not to be flattered and seduced by his teachers and then enlisted in enterprises unworthy of his nature. The true educator will tell him "that there is no sense in him and that he stands in need of it, but that it cannot be acquired unless one works like a slave to attain it" (494d). Plato's teacher, unlike the sophist, is not there only to tend the beast and to utter the sounds that it wishes to hear (493b). His teacher knows which of the beast's desires are beautiful and which are ugly, which good and which evil. For Plato, the truly wise do not spend their time at the doors of the rich (489b), for the same reason that physicians do not go to the ill for advice about health, or navigators to sailors for direction. Contemporary teachers do not enjoy the same confidence in their access to the truth as Plato claimed for his philosopher. Nevertheless we should join him in recognizing that our role as teachers requires us to rigorously challenge the stated beliefs of the young and the assumptions of the society, on which they are based.

SCHOOLING, THE COMMUNITY, AND MORAL EDUCATION

A substantive and perennial problem pervades Plato's *Republic* as well as public debate in our own society. What should the relationship between the school and the society be, in moral education? An intellectual engagement with Plato over this larger issue provides teachers with some needed distance from the debates in our own society. Recently, among those concerned with moral education, there has been a recognition that our recent focus on moral reasoning, and especially its incarnation in the form of the examination of moral dilemmas in classrooms ignores important dimensions of moral growth. Arguing over who may stay and who is to be pushed from the lifeboat does not seem to contribute much to ethical behavior. A renewed concern with the development of character has emerged, along with a recognition of the importance of the community in the shaping of that character. Tensions arise over the teaching of moral issues in schools, and educators argue over the role that moral reasoning plays in character development. I can think of no more powerful way to introduce teachers to the difficult issues of character and community than through the reading and serious discussion of Plato's *Republic*.

A fundamental assumption of the *Republic* is that the community is of overwhelming importance in the creation of character. Plato was convinced that the true philosophical character could not be produced in the sorts of communities with which he was familiar, except by the intervention of God. He wished to start afresh, seeing all aspects of his community as educative, and hence combined the tasks of shaping the community and educating its citizens. His utopianism led to a totalitarianism that most contemporary teachers find objectionable. His descriptions of the different types of societies, anarchy, oligarchy, and democracy, nevertheless, suggest comparisons to our own; and the presentation of his flawed vision of a utopian society challenges us to rethink the ways in which our schools' efforts at moral education are tied to the life of the society of which we are a part.

In Book 6, Plato argues that it is not so much individual teachers, the sophists, who corrupt the young men in the city, as it is the general opinions of the crowd, or the city itself. The crowd makes the young people into the kinds of men and women they want them to be. At public gatherings the crowd applauds some things and objects to others; for Plato, the sophists tend to be swept up in this and to declare the same things to be good and evil, beautiful and ugly, as the crowd does. Further, the crowd has the power to punish and reward the young for their beliefs and actions, thereby further influencing them. "There is not now, has not been in the past, nor ever will be in the future, a man of a character so unusual, that he has been educated to virtue in spite of the education he received from the mob" (497e).

Plato takes seriously the notion that the community educates. There is, for him, little the individual teacher can do to counter the corrupting influence of the city. Hence he creates a utopian society that will educate individuals in an acceptable fashion. Athens argued over what constituted the good life and Plato plunged into the argument. With his descriptions of the four types of cities that have declined from the best sort, and the characters produced in each, Plato acknowledges the variety.

However difficult Plato's task of describing and bringing into being a community that will educate its citizens rightly, our task is even more difficult. We live in the sort of society Plato had in mind when he described a democracy as "full of liberty, and freedom of speech. . . . in it one can do anything one pleases . . . everyone will arrange his

own life in any manner that pleases him" (557b). In Plato's utopian
society, individuals will not arrange their lives as it pleases them. That
is because, in his eyes, not everyone has the wisdom to make such
arrangements. Only the few do, and it is essential that they, and not
those who lack wisdom, make such decisions. They will create the
contours of the society and make the important decisions within it. We
do not tend to place our hopes in philosopher-kings who will annul our
traditions and institutions; our political and educational ideal seems to
be the production of fulfilled individuals and democratic citizens capable of informed participation in the life of the polity. We argue about
the possibility of bringing that ideal into reality and the forms our
educational institutions and practices would take in fulfilling such an
ideal.

We share with Plato a belief that the "best" individuals should
rule our society and that the "best" within each of us should rule the
individual. We seem unwilling, however, to radically reshape our society into an educational state for purposes of securing justice. In fact,
we suspect — and our suspicions are confirmed by reading Plato — that
such an effort at reshaping is likely to have disastrous consequences.
Nor are we willing to accept Plato's noble lie that each of us, born of
the earth, is essentially gold, silver, or bronze, and that most of us are
therefore naturally incapable of moral leadership in society or even of
making wise moral choices for ourselves.

We do not assert that there are no differences in intellectual capacity among individuals, but we seem, at least in our rhetoric, to allow
more power to nurture and less to nature than does Plato, and to leave
the door open for those who come late to the development of intellect.
We also seem less willing to buy into Plato's notion that moral and
political choice is essentially a matter of knowledge, and that hence its
practice requires a degree of expertise similar to that needed for the
practice of medicine. Citizenship is, for us, less a result of formal education and more a product of participation in local political processes.
Unwilling to radically reshape our society and yet recognizing that
Plato was correct in emphasizing the significance of society's values in
shaping the character of individuals, we are faced with the question of
just what role teachers and schools can and ought to play in developing
moral and political leadership. In the *Republic*, education is divided
into two stages. The first is a musical one, including of course drama
and literature, in which young people come to "know" in an imperfect
way how to live their lives. The second stage is open only to those
who have demonstrated a philosophical temperament, good memory,
quickness of mind, and steadfastness of character; these few are put

through a long and arduous process enabling them to know fully various truths and the connections among them.

We will not choose philosopher-kings to shape our society; nor, fortunately, will we be able to start up a new society without historical baggage, or subscribe to any hard-and-fast natural distinctions among human beings. Insofar as our educational work focuses on contributing to the creation of citizens of good character, it will have to include some version of Plato's second stage of education, an education that introduces students to inquiries into the truths behind appearances and to the connections among the truths. But that education will be offered to all students. It will be up to the artfulness of individual teachers how much and how soon they will be able to depart from an earlier musical education intended to shape the character of young children, and begin to introduce them to serious inquiry into the nature of the good life for individuals and society.

Since Plato, we no longer have the option of believing that the way we live as individuals or as a society is a given. How we live our lives is open to inquiry. Moral education, for us, must surely be something more than the consideration of artificial dilemmas, but we cannot allow the teacher's role to be reduced to that of the Sophist in the *Republic*, who teaches nothing "different from the beliefs which the many express whenever they are gathered together, and this he calls wisdom" (493). The enormous part that society plays in the development of the character of its citizens can be challenged by teachers willing to raise questions with their students about the shadows and echoes in the cave.

Colleges, especially schools of education, ought not to be either surprised or embarrassed by the fact that one thing they do well is to study texts. An anxious anti-intellectualism, in its need to do something helpful for the schools, translates the insistence on practicality into a denigration of any intellectual inquiry that is not seen as immediately applicable to specific teaching activities. The importance of practical experience is not an argument against reading and reflecting on significant texts. The experience of the teacher is enriched by the sophistication of the perspective she or he brings to it.

Teachers find in Socrates a man unwilling to accept the assumptions buried either in traditional beliefs or in new ideas. His response to both kinds of ideas is to identify their assumptions, question them, and, through sustained inquiry, measure their worth. Such active and sustained inquiry, which Newman (1976) and others have insisted is the heart of a liberal education, is a crucial need in contemporary teacher education. It is an antidote to two current traps in which teachers and teacher educators, in their efforts to be responsive to social problems, find themselves: They evince a certainty about their own unquestioned beliefs (and an extravagant willingness to impose them on others), and a willingness to carry out teaching practices with little reflection on their worth.

5

LIBERAL EDUCATION AND RESPONSIVENESS TO CURRENT SOCIAL ISSUES

I have been arguing that, to an unfortunate extent, teacher education faculties have embraced too narrow a definition of "practicality" and that the content of their courses has suffered as a result. In this chapter I want to look at another way in which teacher educators have tried to be practical: by joining with the schools in the effort to address significant social problems. The schools have always been expected to solve, or at least to participate in the solution of, significant social problems in this country. They are supposed to reduce inequalities by providing the children of the poor with the skills and attitudes necessary to move up the economic and social ladders. The schools have been seen not only as engines of social mobility but also as guarantors of social order. Since the *Brown v. Board of Education of Topeka, KS* decision, schools throughout the country have been the institutions most deeply involved in the effort to achieve racial integration. Economic inequality and racism are clearly two of the persistent social problems in our society, and the schools are very much a part of efforts to solve them.

I want to narrow my focus, in looking at the schools' role in responding to social problems, to the ways in which teacher educators contribute to the schools' effort to solve social problems through specific curricular changes. The schools have been involved in a broad array of such efforts. Think, for example, in our own day, of mandated sex education courses or units, especially those developed most recently in response to the AIDS crisis; of educational responses to drug and alcohol abuse; or of driver education courses offered in response to safety concerns. Think, too, of the extent to which our high schools reshaped their curricula, in the late nineteenth and early twentieth centuries, to include not only traditional academic preparation for college work but also the preparation of young people for the sorts of tasks they would be expected to perform as members of families and communities and as workers in a changing economy. Recall also the extent to which the schools saw themselves as central to the Americanization of the millions of immigrants who poured into our cities.

It ought not to surprise us that schools in a democratic society have been deeply involved in efforts to address the problems of that society. The extent of local control, for better or worse, guaranteed that the purposes of these schools—and their reflection in the curriculum— would not be the same as those of schools in another time, another place, and a decidedly different economic and social order. America's schools were to be no vestigial organs.

Our educators were ready for the tasks thrust upon them. Whether one thinks of the specifically religious purposes of schools in seventeenth-century Massachusetts, or of the New England schoolmistress gone west to tame the Huck Finns of the frontier towns, or gone south to teach the newly freed slaves, or of the teachers in our eastern cities who thought it their duty to introduce to the children of poor immigrants a Protestant middle-class morality, one sees everywhere this perception of a moral purpose among the teaching profession. Add to this moral purpose the American confidence in our ability to shape the natural environment and the human social order, and the belief that the schools are the institution through which this shaping can best take place, and we have a mixture that, while possessing extraordinary energy, also threatens to overreach itself. The schools take on too many tasks, at some of which they prove incompetent, and they intrude into the lives of students in ways that, on reflection, seem inappropriate in a democratic society.

Teacher educators have shown a particular interest in encouraging teachers to take on these large tasks in their work. To some extent, this is simply because we have ourselves been inducted into progressive educational traditions that have emphasized the school's role in creating a better society; but it is also because we teacher educators, or some of us at least, are teachers in search of a subject matter. We tend not to see ourselves as masters of a specialized discipline into which we are inducting young people, but rather as teachers in a seminary preparing missionaries to go out into a difficult world and save the souls of the young. The focus is on what the young will become, and on the extent to which what they become will contribute to creating a better society. As participants in the progressive tradition, teacher educators tend not to define the purpose of schools in terms of imparting a body of knowledge, encapsulated in a set of readings, but instead to ask: What are the real-life problems that society will face, and how can we help teachers to make the school curriculum responsive to those problems?

A progressive view of education sees all experience as educative; defines intelligence not as a collection of principles existing prior to experience but as an active grappling with new experience; and sees knowledge not as belonging to a small elite but as flowing through all of society and gaining in power from that distribution. Proponents of this view must take care that educational progressivism not be captured by an anti-intellectual band of moralists, who, using the techniques of the behaviorists, interpret the progressive effort to use the schools for individual and social betterment as an intrusive shaping of children's behavior toward specific "desirable" ends.

Teacher educators have been deeply involved in two recent efforts to address social problems through changes in school curriculum and practice: moral education and multicultural education. What sort of teacher education will preserve a commitment to addressing these important issues in schools, and yet at the same time protect teachers from an overreaching moralism that neglects intellectual inquiry into the complexity of the issues addressed?

MORAL EDUCATION

An interest in moral education is hardly unique to this moment in the history of American schooling. No society's education has been without a significant moral dimension, and, in fact, it is difficult to separate the moral dimension of education from its other purposes. Nevertheless, the present heightened interest in moral education appears to stem from a definable set of conditions that themselves limit the nature of the moral education our public schools may offer.

We have taken the notion of individual freedom seriously and, in developing as a nation, have witnessed the erosion of various types of communities — villages and small towns, religious and ethnic groups — that had been the transmitters of moral values. Of the Americans living today, many did not grow up in communities that inducted them into a predetermined way of life. People have options. Many of us thought that freedom of choice was quite a good thing. We didn't want our lives defined by the values of the religious or ethnic group or small town into which we had been born. The limitations that these communities placed on us were stifling, so we took a train and headed for the big city. There, in anonymity, we were free to make our choices, but for some of us they turned out badly.

Many see the social chaos around us as the product of the uprooted individualism I have just described, and have called for the public schools to engage in the teaching of values to a new generation in the hope of reversing the evils they see in the society about them. I think they oversimplify in blaming all of our social ills on the diminishing power of communities to transmit values, but they do call to our attention an important tension between our love of individualism and freedom and our nostalgia for a time in which we lived more rooted lives (Grant, 1988).

It is precisely that tension which sets the stage for my argument about the sort of education needed to prepare teachers to engage in moral education today. Since we no longer live in a world where the school is an extension of a strong and unified community, we cannot expect teachers to transmit an agreed-upon set of values as if they were describing the way the world is and inducting people into it. Teachers who attempt to do so will be misleading students. We do not live in the sort of society in which we can say: This is how you fish; this is what it is to be a wife or a warrior; this is the role you shall play in our community (MacIntyre, 1981).

The teacher's tasks in our society are far more complex because for some time we have been raising questions about what constitutes the good life. In fact, the teacher's role in moral education is not a given and is, therefore, like other roles in the society, subject to inquiry and redefinition. As thoughtful teacher educators, we should not simply tell teachers what values they are to pass on and provide them with techniques to effect the transmission; our task is far more difficult.

In teacher education there is a tendency to package things such as moral education. This tendency takes the form of a search for specific directions ("These are the steps we must follow, this is what teachers need to know about moral education in order to function in classrooms"). We might call this a technical as opposed to a liberal approach. It seems clear that in moral education, an approach more closely aligned with a liberal education is needed. Much of what teachers learn that is relevant to moral education will not necessarily be learned under the rubric "moral education." Much of what they learn will not be immediately or directly applicable to their teaching. Educating teachers requires a commitment to the notion that rational inquiry into the larger context of issues like moral education is a worthwhile activity. We need to escape the anxiety of immediate applicability, and to embrace the patience of understanding the contexts in which educational practice goes on.

What an extraordinarily complex matter moral education turns out to be! Teachers will find all sorts of claims about what it is, and a variety of directions for how they should go about it. A teacher's education should echo this complexity and encourage the development of a perspective from which to analyze the various conflicting claims and directions. Some believe that there is a nucleus of moral and political beliefs to which all of us subscribe. There is no little irony in the fact that they assert this even as they decry the moral and social chaos they see around them. In seeking a moral consensus, they assert a democratic rationale for its existence. In a joint statement offered by the American Federation of Teachers, the Educational Excellence Network, and Freedom House, the authors set out a list of core beliefs to which they feel everyone can subscribe: "Devotion to human dignity and freedom, to equal rights, to social and economic justice, to the rule of law, to civility and truth, to tolerance and diversity, to personal and civic responsibility, to self-restraint and self-respect — all these must be taught and learned and practiced" (Education for Democracy, 1987, p. 8). Here we have a list of values that teachers are to transmit to students. It is difficult, though clearly not impossible, to argue against any one of them. They do seem to be a set of core values to which we can all subscribe, but in the end the list does not seem very helpful for teachers. When we look closely at the concrete circumstances surrounding moral decisions affected by these values, significant differences between individuals emerge. And it is, of course, precisely such concrete circumstances that teachers engaged in moral education examine with their students. The asserted moral consensus was purchased at the price of remaining at a level of abstraction inappropriate to the education of young people. What specific forms ought our commitment to tolerance and diversity take? When we ask such questions, and others even more closely tied to concrete circumstances, our assumed moral consensus collapses. The task of the teacher and of teacher educators becomes more complex.

There are those who urge teachers to cease trying to inculcate in students any particular set of values, and to teach them instead how to make intelligent inquiries into moral issues. Israel Scheffler, for example, states flatly:

> To choose the democratic ideal for society is wholly to reject the conception of education as an instrument of rule; it is to surrender the idea of shaping or molding the mind of the pupil. The function of education in a democracy is rather to liberate the mind, to strengthen its critical powers, inform it with knowledge and the capacity for critical inquiry, engage its human sympathies, and illuminate its moral and practical choices. (1983, p. 311)

Scheffler's conception of how we should undertake moral education is rooted in his notion of educational purpose. Other philosophers of education have joined him in urging a rational approach to moral education that, by and large, seeks to avoid a commitment to a particular set of moral ideals and stresses, instead, the teaching of thinking processes appropriate to moral inquiry.

But clearly the philosophers have given teachers no easy way out. One cannot learn a set of rules for thinking about moral issues and apply them in classrooms. Philosophers argue over the very possibility of making meaningful moral claims. Teachers who wish to lead inquiries into moral issues will have to gain some sense of what constitute appropriate inquiry strategies. Most of us will characterize our own moral arguments as rational, but in making such claims we may be hiding from both ourselves and others the pursuit of our own interests. The teacher who claims to be rational and objective may be neither. It is not only individual self-interest that leads us to think we are being rational when we are not; the terms of debate on the great issues of the day are often not set by individual rational inquirers but by powerful interests in the society. A teacher's education will have to include philosophical inquiry into the nature of moral reasoning as well as sociological understandings of the origins of the "common sense" of the society. Teachers will have to learn a great deal about the significant moral issues in their society and develop a capacity to identify and question their own assumptions. This can happen only when we conceive of moral education, not as a limited area over which teachers are to gain a technical mastery suitable for classroom application, but as part of a broader liberal education. We then create an opportunity for teachers to bring a genuinely reflective power to the specific issues of moral education in classrooms.

A variety of arguments about moral education persist among teacher educators. Much has been said, for example, of the stress on rationality in the general ethical theories of the last two centuries and, more specifically, in theories of moral education. The argument is that we have overemphasized ethical principles and logical inquiry in our concern for the justification of rights or of individual action. We have viewed moral education as solving moral dilemmas, as training in an essentially cognitive process. In so doing, we have neglected the affective elements of caring and concern. More recently, this argument has been linked to the notion of gender-specific ways of knowing (see Sichel, 1988, pp. 167–224). The argument surely has merit and implies that in the process of teacher education we will want to examine questions about those aspects of human beings, aside from the rational, which are involved in moral activity, and the extent to which those aspects might be implicated in a program of moral education.

Others remind us that one initially learns morality not by focusing on methods of inquiry into moral dilemmas but by induction into the habits and practices of a particular moral tradition. They claim that the moral character so produced has a stronger influence on behavior than does any later cognitive training received in a classroom. Teachers will want to inquire as to just what relationship the encouragment of rational inquiry might have to this kind of character development, which has taken place in the historical communities to which individuals belong. Further, when individual students seem to lack this character formation, the question arises: Can the schools themselves form communities that will contribute to the development of character? Again, the business of educating moral educators involves much more than training in the use of some particular set of materials; the complexities of the issues I am outlining call for a long-term commitment to intellectual inquiry on the part of teachers, and for an effort on the part of teacher educators to see their work as part and parcel of the work of liberal education.

It is clear, too, that certain psychological and social conditions are necessary in order for young people to reach a point where we might describe their behavior as moral. The capacity for moral inquiry and action is tied to a "healthy" upbringing. The teacher's approach to moral education must therefore include an understanding of the ways in which the presence or absence of key early childhood experiences impinges on moral development. And teachers must also be aware of the present psychological strengths and weaknesses of their pupils. Students are more than mere cognitive machines, and, even if teachers defined their fundamental interest in students as a cognitive one, in the pursuit of cognitive goals they would have to take into consideration their students' other dimensions. Teachers will have to learn to conduct classroom inquiries that encourage students to speak openly on moral issues, to examine the merit of their own claims and the claims of others, and at the same time to preserve and strengthen their egos so that they can continue to engage in moral inquiry and activity.

Some in our society make a strong argument for the notion that the public schools ought to stay out of the business of moral education altogether. Those who adopt this hands-off stance point out that the values the public schools teach over the years may change, or may vary from one part of the country to the other. Either the moral majority or the secular humanists may have control of the schools; the hands-off position does not itself offer a program of moral education, but simply asks the schools as agents of the state to stick to the business of teaching facts and skills and to stay away from moral education. It rejects the claim that we are only teaching the process of inquiry in moral education and not a particular moral content.

Teachers who would engage in moral education, then, not only have an extraordinarily complex set of issues to address as they pursue their own education, but they must operate knowing that society has raised serious questions about the very legitimacy of the task in which they are engaged. Should a free society forbid its schools to engage in moral education? Are there limitations on the nature of the moral education that a free society might offer in its schools? Is it realistic to expect the schools to embark on moral programs with such limits? Is the legitimacy of the teacher's role in pursuing moral education affected by the manner in which the content and process of that education are determined? Are there limits on a moral education program devised by a democratic decision-making process? What is the appropriate relationship between the professionally trained teacher and the community in the area of moral education? These issues must be addressed in the course of a teacher's education.

One argument against those who question the right of the public schools to engage in moral education is that the schools cannot, even if they wish to, avoid the transmission of moral values. The subject matter emphasized, motivation and grading practices, extracurricular activities, the organizational realities of the school, teacher behaviors toward students, the style of group activities — these and many other factors in the life of a school create a moral climate that has a greater effect on students than any conscious program of moral development. If the argument has merit — and I believe it does — then the education of teachers who will engage in moral education cannot focus simply on exchanges between teacher and student, but must encourage teachers to look seriously at the role of the school climate. Of course, if we are to take this sociological dimension seriously in talking about the task of educating teachers, then we may want teachers to look at the moral climate of the larger society, especially as that climate affects school purposes and practices, and especially as teachers themselves, often unwittingly, become the mediators of a society's values to young people.

Although most religious groups in this country have established an uneasy truce with public education, calling only for more recognition of religion in the schools, some join in the belief that the public schools should leave moral education to the family and to the religious communities into which individuals are born (Johnson, 1980; McCarthy, Skillen, & Harper, 1982). These groups are often alienated from what they perceive as the mainstream values of the society, and by extension from public schools and public school teachers as the presumable embodiers and transmitters of those values. Different religious groups are upset about different issues. Some focus on the general materialism of the society, others on nuclear arms policy, still others on sexual morality. Teachers need to understand the connections between the rise of public schools and the development of a secular morality. They need to understand also why some religious leaders, at least, are concerned about the advancement of a civil religion that could be enacted in the schools.

Moral education involves an extraordinarily complex set of questions and controversies about whether and how it ought to be conducted in our society. Its nature argues against any effort to reduce it to a curriculum package for teachers or a set of techniques to be mastered. Only a continuum of general and professional courses designed to encourage critical reflection by teachers on these larger issues makes sense.

MULTICULTURAL EDUCATION

Of late, schools of education have been urged to evince in their programs an understanding of the multicultural realities of our society (Gay, 1986). As with moral education, it is possible to trace part of the interest in multicultural education to the problems of society and to educators' desire to help solve those problems. To understate the well-known case: Blacks, Hispanics, Native Americans, and other minority racial and ethnic groups are overrepresented among the poor, the powerless, and the unemployed. At least some of this overrepresentation is due to racism in the dominant white society. One purpose of multicultural education is to alter racist attitudes. Furthermore, the schools are viewed as institutions through which individuals can acquire the skills and attitudes needed to move out of poverty. But minority groups are also overrepresented among those who drop out of schools. Hence proponents of multicultural education seek to identify curricular, pedagogical, and institutional changes that will encourage these groups to succeed in school. Finally, there is a growing realization that the history and literature we have been teaching in our schools is itself the product of a narrow ethnocentrism and that we need to move toward multiple understandings of our past.

As with moral education, it would be a mistake to reify multicultural education, to see it as a unit, course, or program that teacher candidates must pass through as part of their training. Nor can we train teachers in a set of specific behaviors. What we can do is deepen their knowledge of the complexities of issues of race and class in our society, introduce them to the ways in which knowledge is constructed, and encourage them to explore the educational implications of these matters for their own schools and classrooms.

Learning Styles

A currently much-discussed issue within multiculturalism is the claim that students from different cultural groups have different learning styles and therefore should be taught differently (Anderson, 1988). The claim is often accompanied by the argument that minority youths' lack of school success and high dropout rate are due in part to a mismatch between the ways in which teachers ordinarily expect students to learn and the culturally specific learning styles of minority group members.

The claim is not implausible. If individuals are socialized within different cultures, differences in learning style should come as no surprise. But surely the task of teacher education is not to begin identifying relevant cultural differences and specifying how teachers might alter their approaches in response to these differences. This is a recipe-like approach into which teacher educators have been drawn on many other issues. We want teachers to inquire into wider contexts and concerns. For example, they will need to consider the argument that treating students alike unless there is a pedagogically relevant reason for treating them differently would seem to be a defensible democratic and equalitarian principle. To argue for the differential treatment of different groups one would have to make a strong case that the students involved would indeed benefit from the differential treatment. Further, individual differences among students would seem to have a stronger claim to differential educational treatment than group differences, simply because generalizations made about any group are unlikely to be true of all of its members. Historically, minority groups have been treated differently, and to their detriment, based on assumed differences in abilities. Assertions about differences in learning styles may be intended to point up learning strengths in particular groups, but they can easily become a two-edged sword. These are not simple issues, and my argument is that a genuine teacher education will address them rather than operate from a set of assumptions that assumes no further inquiry into them is needed.

Further discussion of the claim that different cultural groups should be taught differently because they have different cognitive styles may be more fruitful if we look at some concrete descriptions of these reported differences. The learning differences are usually seen as embedded in a larger world view specific to a culture. Some studies have shown differences in perspective and depth perception among groups. Other studies claim that some groups learn disjunctive concepts more easily than conjunctive ones; are more field-dependent than others during classification tasks; incorporate more affective and subjective elements into their inquiries and judgments, or better integrate cognitive and affective approaches in their learning styles; are more motivated to work within a cooperative than a competitive setting; do better at analytic tasks (while other groups do better at holistic ones); or are more responsive to explicit and detailed direction, as opposed to indirection and suggestion (Anderson, 1988, p. 6).

Supposing such claims to be true, what sorts of instructional responses might teachers make to them? While some claim that "There is no such thing as one style being better than the other" (Anderson, 1988, p. 6), it would seem fair to say that one style may be better suited to some tasks than others. We ought not to deprive any group of the opportunity to practice a variety of learning approaches. Further, there may be normative reasons why teachers should choose one motivational strategy rather than another, reasons that at some point should be given more weight than the practices of a particular cultural group. Listen to Sleeter and Grant (1987):

> The previous learning experiences of many Southeast Asian refugees were likely to have been by rote; students listened and then repeated on tests verbatim what had been presented in classes. Hmong-American students, therefore, may well need to learn to ask questions, to use creative thinking skills, and to participate in the class. (p. 425)

Here, certain educational values, such as "creative thinking skills" and "class participation," are seen as worthwhile enough to be encouraged in students whose culture does not emphasize them.

More typically, proponents of multicultural education point up cultural differences in order to encourage teachers to use motivational and instructional devices that capitalize on the ongoing cultural property of the group, and to avoid instructional and motivational strategies that run counter to the group's values.

> White middle class values generally encourage competition, winning, and efforts to achieve status and prestige. While minority individuals may

also appreciate status and prestige, some groups, including many Native Americans, emphasize instead the value of cooperative effort. Some Native American children have even been known to wait until all their classmates have finished their assignment before raising their hands in unison, thereby preventing anyone the embarrassment of being last. Many Mexican-American students are taught by their parents that when they achieve competitively, it is at the expense of their peers. It is better, therefore, to avoid competition than to have someone else, perhaps a friend or relative, suffer from any advantages gained through competing. (Chinn, undated)

Here, teachers are urged not to interpret an unwillingness to compete as lack of motivation, and in other places they are urged to use cooperation rather than competition as a motivational device. Thus the teacher must make difficult choices about which practices of the cultural group are to be challenged or supplemented, and which practices should be reinforced and even presented as ideals to be emulated by others.

Preparing teachers to work in a multicultural society is clearly not as simple as identifying a definable learning style for each group and inventing assignments, motivational strategies, and other aspects of the educational environment in response to it. Banks has sketched out the complexities of the learning styles issue (1988) and of multiculturalism in general (1993). A liberal teacher education can provide opportunities for teachers to explore the political, pedagogogical, and normative dimensions of such issues and should avoid specifying behaviors in which teachers ought to engage.

Teachers should familiarize themselves with the literature on cultural differences, reading it with a critical eye and attempting to assess whether such differences warrant efforts on their part to alter their own classroom practices. Observation of how such changes work with individual students is clearly in order, as is concern lest the shifts in teaching approaches result in some groups' being deprived of the opportunity to exercise valuable skills. There are differences in the ways in which people go about making sense of their world, and some of these ways are associated with culture. But there is a whole set of matters that teachers viewing these differences will have to take into account as they decide whether to rely on a particular learning strength in their students or to supplement that strength by encouraging other learning approaches. Nor should we fall back on cultural reasons at every turn to explain differences in student performance.

Much of American literature depicts the painful clash between the children of immigrants, who are determinedly becoming Americans, and their parents, who are seen as representing an older way of life (Rodriguez, 1982). The younger generation is often depicted as inventing itself culturally while attempting to succeed economically, often in flight from the visible markings of the older culture (e.g., its clothes, gestures, language, food). However much we may desire that such painful transitions not occur, however much we may desire that one be able to live a successful life in this country without sacrificing a previous cultural identity, we should be careful about assigning to individuals traits that they may in fact be in the process of changing.

More than just differences in learning style are at stake in multicultural education. The concern with learning styles grows out of the recognition that schools are often seen as unwelcoming or even hostile to minority groups, and that such perceptions account, in part, for lack of success and for dropping out. How students can be made to feel welcome, and how the school can be made a place in which their cultural identity is celebrated and not diminished, are questions that go beyond the issue of learning styles and point to the need for reflection on a whole set of individual and institutional practices.

The normative aspect of the educational enterprise is inescapable. Teachers must decide whether the use of competition or cooperation is a better motivational tool in a particular context, and they must realize that the choice of a motivational tool is not only a teaching strategy to be judged on its effectiveness in producing some learning outcome, but also a part of the curriculum of values that the student is learning. The same may be said of the choice between rote learning and active participation. Neither an unthinking certainty about habitual ways of doing things nor a shabby relativism, which asserts that one choice is as good as another, should be allowed to substitute for an examination of the context within which the teaching situation takes place. Teachers who make such choices because that is the way they have always done things, or because now they have been told to be responsive to the learning styles of particular ethnic groups, fail to grasp the need for informed reflection on a complex problem. In educating teachers, we can provide no formulas, only an induction into the kind of thinking and practice that good teaching involves, and the continued support of such thinking and practice.

Curricular Changes

Teachers, increasingly, are involved in the curriculum-making process. Rarely are they in the position of starting from scratch and asking: "What knowledge is of most worth?" They do find themselves, however, on textbook selection committees; they often individually select materials for their own classes; they participate in school or district reviews of grade or course content; they are involved in reevaluations of teaching approaches in a particular subject area sponsored by professional groups; and, of course, in the assignments they give and in the discussions they lead in classes, they directly affect the curricular experiences of learners. A sound teacher education will encourage reflection on the significance of multicultural realities for curriculum development.

Besides the cognitive development of children, the schools have traditionally been charged with the task of celebrating and sustaining the values of the community of which they are a part. The cognitive and celebratory functions of schooling have often been intertwined; the schools teach what happened in history at the same time as they point up the heroic accomplishments of members of the community of which they are a part and shape the story to enhance the community's sense of its place in the world. They treat literature not only from an esthetic or literary perspective but also as an embodiment of the hopes and values of the society. Multicultural reformers argue that the community whose values we have been celebrating has been defined too narrowly. Various ethnic groups and women have been ignored in the development of history and literature curricula, or their role in history has been distorted, reflecting the values of those in power in the society (McKay, 1987). This exclusion and distortion has the effect on women and on ethnic groups of undermining their identity. Some members of the community are not only not celebrated, they are invisible or are presented in demeaning ways.

The problem, however, is not only the impact of the distorted curriculum on the various excluded groups but also its impact on those who identify with the group that has defined the curriculum. Their perceptions of themselves and of others are limited by the ethnocentric curriculum to which they have been exposed. The main barrier that multicultural educational reformers face is that those in power do not see the standard curriculum as ethnocentric; they see it as objective or as reflective of common values. They take the "mainstream" curriculum for granted and may view the introduction of a female or black author into a course as a departure in need of justification. Such disputes about curriculum have the effect of calling to our attention the extent to which curriculum is not at all a given, but a social construction, one that reflects historical shifts in power within the society. Arthur Schlesinger (1991) sees the multiculturalists as promoting ethnic pride at the cost of historical truth; surely some do this. What Schlesinger fails to point out is that all nations, including our own, have enlisted school history curricula in propaganda efforts; historical truth has always taken a back seat to nation-building.

What, then, is needed in a teacher education that is to prepare teachers to work in a multicultural society? What does it take to produce the cosmopolitanism and sophistication needed by teachers participating in curriculum change in this multicultural society? As with moral education, we can conceive of no short cuts, such as training in the dissemination of a particular curriculum. What seems necessary, instead, is an understanding of the social construction of the curriculum and the relation of that curriculum to the historical and political realities of our society. Studying curriculum-making in another society, and its relation to the political and cultural values in that society, would provide teachers with a better understanding of how knowledge and values transmission works (Stock-Morton, 1988). The historical examination of the ways in which the curriculum of America's schools has changed in response to changes in the larger society can provide teachers with a sense that what they teach has always been open to alteration (Fitzgerald, 1979; Kliebard, 1986).

Teachers of history and literature, especially, will need to become familiar with a wider variety of texts that incorporate previously ignored perspectives and are appropriate to their area or grade level — no small task. And they will need to address the tension between the celebration of differences and the desire to create a shared culture in the nation. In discussions of multicultural education, emotions and polemics often outstrip carefully considered examination of the issues. Added to the blindness of those in power to their own ethnocentrism is the willingness of some calling for new approaches to curriculum to sacrifice careful inquiry to the installation of a new orthodoxy. Teachers will be responsible for the forms that new curricula take. Broadly-educated teachers will use primarily educational criteria in their approach to teaching. They will begin to introduce their students to arguments over what happened in history and over contemporary meanings of past events, as well as to the ways in which historians go about making inquiries. Their focus will be on enhancing the learner's capacity to inquire into the truth, not on espousing any orthodoxy, new or old.

Concerns with moral and multicultural education are among the forms that the effort to use the schools as a tool in the creation of a better society has taken in our day. The willingness of the progressive education tradition and of progressivism generally to use institutions of the state to create a better society has unfortunately been marred by a translation of those social concerns into an effort to manage the behavior of individuals toward desirable ends. Teachers have been viewed as junior executives in this management of virtue, in the shaping of individuals and society by those who know "better." Teachers will remain a part of this moralistic-technocratic approach only as long as their own education continues to be insistently narrow, centered on training in skills that are seen as necessary to produce the sorts of individuals and society we desire.

I am calling here for a way of educating teachers that will produce, not assistant managers trained in a set of tasks to be accomplished, but autonomous human beings capable of continuing inquiry into school purposes and practices — and, crucially, capable of inviting students to inquire into the conditions and purposes of their own lives. When teachers are assigned "tasks" such as moral education and multicultural education, it is foolish to lay out a program for them to follow, to train them in a set of behaviors to accomplish these tasks, or even to specify what sorts of behaviors will be needed. Preparing teachers to engage in moral and multicultural education turns out to be remarkably like preparing human beings to live with the complexities of the modern world. Insofar as intellectual inquiry — serious writing and thinking — can help one to live in that world, so too can it help to prepare teachers for that world's classrooms.

6

METHODS AND STUDENT TEACHING: LIBERAL AND TECHNICAL DIMENSIONS

Nothing defines teacher education in the eyes of those outside of it so much as the methods course and the teaching practice that follows it. If teacher education has any legitimate role at all, from this viewpoint, it is to teach would-be teachers how to teach. One becomes well educated in one's subject matter and then picks up a few techniques and practices them; the new teacher has learned the "what to teach" part and now needs to learn "how to teach." These are perfectly normal ways of talking about teaching, and the concepts involved are somewhat useful; at times it makes sense to talk about the "how" and the "what" of teaching as if they were separate from each other. However, like most ways of categorizing complex behavior, such distinctions can also be misleading.

Students preparing to teach in the elementary schools ought to take methods courses in the various subject areas in which they will be teaching, and those preparing to teach in the secondary schools ought to take a methods course in the subject they will be teaching. Some serious thinking about the relationship between the "how" and the "what" of teaching, ought, however, to inform the design of these courses.

It makes sense that certain courses should focus on the "how" of teaching. What doesn't make sense is the belief that the "how" of teaching a given subject consists of a body of prescriptions that is separate from the subject under consideration, from our general understandings of life, from our thinking about learning and educational purpose, and from our specific knowledge of the students in a class. What the education faculty needs least from the liberal arts people is uninformed criticism; what they need most is the infusion of the spirit of a liberal education into their own courses. If, in fact, the methods of teaching any subject area are connected to these other understandings, then the learning of methods becomes not just a technical enterprise but a richly textured and complex one. The focus stays on the "how to," but the "how to" and the actual doing force us to ask all sorts of significant questions in new and more pressing ways about the enterprise of teaching subject matter to students.

TEACHING QUESTIONING TECHNIQUES

Let me illustrate my general point with the example of "questioning," an important topic in methods courses and textbooks, and one which supervisors of student teachers often address in their conferences with student teachers. In the 1950s Benjamin Bloom (1956) developed a taxononomy of educational objectives that has enormously affected the way in which educational theorists and even some teachers think about teaching and learning. He divided educational objectives into three areas: the cognitive, affective, and psycho-motor domains. In the cognitive domain, he listed six levels of objectives: knowledge, comprehension, application, analysis, synthesis, and evaluation.

Bloom's categories have been adapted for a variety of purposes, including as a classification system for teacher questions. Theorists argue that if you want students to engage in appropriate intellectual behaviors, then you have to ask them the sorts of questions that will prompt those behaviors. The genius of the taxonomy was that it gave teachers a vocabulary with which to talk about their own behavior and that of their students. Trained observers could watch teachers and chart the frequency with which they engaged in various sorts of questioning behavior. This method provided more objective feedback than might otherwise be possible. Observers also studied the sorts of responses engendered in the students by questioning at different levels.

The prescriptive possibilities of the taxonomy are obvious. Those in the various subject areas who urged an inquiry approach to teaching had a marvelous tool in Bloom's category system. If the teacher thought it was important that students engage, at least some of the time, in higher-order thinking, then the teacher would benefit from training in asking higher-order questions. These categories show up in a variety of methods texts published in the 1970s and 1980s.

Beginning with a presentation of Bloom's categories in their science methods text for elementary school teachers—in a chapter entitled "How Can You Improve Your Questioning and Listening Skills?"—Arthur Carin and Robert Sund (1989) move to their own claims that "science processes are the backbone of a science program for elementary school children. They are the ways in which we help children use, on their own maturation levels, the processes that scientists use" (p. 159).

They then offer a chart with critical thinking processes in one column and an example of a question meant to prompt each thinking process in a column beside it. Thus, predicting or hypothesizing behavior is prompted by the question "What do you think will happen if more salt is added to the oceans next year?" Similarly, "What conclusions can you make from the experiment information?" cues students to make inferences, interpret data, or draw conclusions. More directly, "How would you group these buttons?" encourages classifying behavior. Interestingly, the teacher is here asked to take the focus off her own performance, and to look at the sorts of behaviors she is trying to encourage in her students. Here Carin favors using the processes that scientists themselves use (1989, p. 159).

In a popular social studies elementary text, in a chapter entitled "Encouraging Inquiry," John Jarolimek (1977) also bases his discussion on Bloom's taxonomy. "In terms of inquiry the most important questions to ask are those that require elaborate reflective responses. These higher level questions often begin, 'Why . . . ,' 'How . . . ,' 'How do we know . . . ,' 'Show that . . . ,' 'If that is true, then . . . '" (p. 127). Jarolimek says that such questions trigger responses that are

> in accord with a problem-solving, discovery learning format. When a child is presented with certain information and then asked why an area has a small population, she is being cued into certain high-level thinking processes. Simply recalling a "correct" response is not adequate—the information has to be processed intellectually: analyzed, synthesized, applied, interpreted, evaluated and so on. (pp. 127–128)

Here, the question-asking strategy is related to ideas about effective learning. In his discussion of questioning techniques in *Social Studies for the Twenty-First Century: Methods and Materials for Teaching in Middle and Secondary Schools*, Jack Zevin (1992) also uses Bloom's taxonomy.

Two other techniques associated with question-asking frequently find their way into discussions of teaching methods. The first, of older vintage, is rooted in the distinction between convergent and divergent questions, and the second is the more limited but helpful notion of "wait time." Carin and Sund (1989) use both of these concepts in their methods book. They define the notions of convergent and divergent questions: "Open or divergent questions are those that encourage a broad range of diverse responses. . . . Closed or convergent questions . . . focus on specific, teacher acceptable answers" (pp. 152–153). They go on to tell the fledgling teacher what purposes are best served by each type. They offer a list of sample questions and categorize each, explaining their categorization. They then report on Mary Budd Rowe's work on "wait time." She found that all sorts of pedagogically desirable things happen when teachers increase their wait time from 1 to 3 seconds. For example, the length and number of responses increase. The number of questions asked by students increases. Finally, achievement in complex items on written tests improves.

I think it fair to classify each of the above strategies—levels of questioning, convergent and divergent questions, and wait time—as techniques. I habitually use them in my college classroom and, importantly, would not have used them to any great extent had I not been made aware of the concepts through the educational literature and the discussions that follow publication of such ideas. These techniques are widely cited in methods texts and courses. The most important task of the methods teacher, and of those preparing to teach various subjects at various levels, is to integrate these questioning techniques with larger understandings of the matter and method of their subject, with their understandings of the students in their classes and of themselves, and with broader understandings of how the world works.

Questioning and the Nature of the Subject

Look at the intellectual complexity into which we step, if we take ourselves seriously, when we begin constructing questions for our students. Arthur Carin tells me (personal communication, April 1991) that he will have to revise some of his suggestions on questioning in the next edition of his book as a result of the work of Rosalind Driver (1986). She argues that the conceptual schemes children bring to their experiences make it unlikely that they will derive the appropriate generalizations when presented with inquiry materials. This makes the textbook writer's and teacher's task more complex. Recall what Carin writes in his methods text for teachers of elementary school science, echoing Jerome Bruner (1960) and others: The object is to induct the students into science processes, to set them on the road to acting like scientists. Thus, we ask questions that involve the students in these processes. Now, surely there are generic processes in which all scientists participate, processes that take different forms depending on the sort of work a scientist does. Just as surely, there are approaches to reality, conceptual structures, typical questions, that are peculiar to different sciences. The biologist asks a different set of questions than the physicist. So if one wishes to engage students, at some level, in the work of the various sciences, if one wishes to construct questions that prompt students to do the work of the physicist or biologist, one must know what sorts of questions these people ask and what sort of work they do. This is no easy task. It calls for a preparatory education in subject matter that includes a meta-dimension, an effort to understand the sorts of inquiries the biologist or the physicist makes. Teachers, then, will likely be better questioners if they have not only mastered a vocabulary like Bloom's, with its hierarchy of questioning and cognitive objectives, but also developed a sophisticated understanding of the nature and purpose of the work in the field they are teaching. One function of a methods course in the teaching of science might be a synthetic one, helping the teacher to understand the sorts of questions and processes that are typical of the various sciences. This is precisely what is called for in college-level science courses by those who feel that science is generally taught in colleges in too specialized a fashion, and without providing any intellectual context. The purposes of those who wish to design science courses as part of a liberal education coincide here with the purposes of those seeking to design science courses for teachers.

The complexities that might appropriately be addressed in a methods course abound. For example, practitioners in different subject areas may argue over the nature and purpose of their work, and teachers in elementary and secondary schools may have purposes in teaching their subjects beyond inducting students into the work of practitioners in the field.

If an English teacher were to decide to model his questioning of students on the questions literary critics and theorists ask of literature, he would be faced with a wide array of choices. The critics and theorists, who certainly share some commonalities, nevertheless quarrel with one another over what sorts of questions ought to be asked about literature. Similarly, contemporary social scientists argue over appropriate methods of inquiry in their field. There is much discussion over the role of empirical methods and quantification, over the need for the inquirer to examine her own assumptions and the assumptions of the culture from within which she is working, and over newer ethnographic approaches to data collection and interpretation. The historians, too, argue—over methods of inquiry, over questions of meaning in history, over whether to focus on kings and queens, wars and nations, or on the fabric of everyday life. They question their own ability to speak in terms of cause and effect, to give voice to those previously ignored, and to make judgments about historical individuals and events.

Thus, English or social studies teachers, focusing on the nature of the subject area they are teaching, find that the appropriateness of the questions they will ask students is itself problematic. They are forced to take seriously questions about the nature of the subject matter they are teaching by their efforts to determine "how" they ought to teach it. The "how" question is, then, more than just a matter of accumulating a bag of tricks or a set of techniques (in this case, techniques of questioning). The methods course is forced into the larger debate about the nature of the subject being taught. Such a focus is, as we have seen, an appropriate part of a liberal education.

Questioning and Educational Purpose

Teachers may construct questions that strike practitioners within a subject field, such as historians or physicists, as irrelevant. That is because teachers' purposes are not derived solely from within a discipline. Significant writings about educational purpose often mention such goals as self-awareness, moral development, and citizenship. Thus, since Plato, teachers have been concerned about the impact of portrayals of character and action in literature on young people. English teachers in our day are less likely to use characters in literature as direct models for or warnings to their students, but they do ask questions designed to encourage students to think about their own moral development. Teachers may ask questions about the use of irony in *Macbeth*, but they also may ask about student attitudes toward ambition or guilt, moving from the play into the moral lives of the students. At their best, English teachers try to tie questions that help students to understand the work of literature at hand to questions focused on self-understanding.

Social studies and history teachers are expected, in most statements of educational purpose, to play some role in forming good citizens. Just what shape this purpose will take in teacher questions and assignments seems, again, problematic. Serious teachers, debating what sort of questions to ask of their students to move them toward good citizenship, are driven back to fundamental questions about their own role and about what sort of citizens they hope to develop. Again, the apparently technical issue of questioning procedures leads the teacher into much larger questions.

Questioning and the Understanding of Self, Students, and the World

Teachers' dealings with students in classrooms are not only the product of a set of learned skills but the outgrowth of self-understanding. Those teachers who work at the task of self-understanding in relation to their work in classrooms obviously increase their chances for success. This sort of self-knowledge clearly has a cognitive dimension to it. But it seems much more difficult to learn things about ourselves than to learn information that has little effect on our own emotional lives. Learning to be a teacher includes learning about those aspects of the self that impinge on one's teaching and developing a willingness to alter behaviors even when we might have an emotional investment in sustaining them.

To illustrate my point, I will quote at some length here from an essay written by a student teacher in response to a set of questions from me. The student teacher was a 40-year-old man who had come to teaching after working in other areas.

> After my first week of student teaching I was speaking to my aunt (who, by the way, is a nun), and she asked me how my students were behaving. "I've got them under control," I answered. I wonder if it's my grandfather in me? . . . My grandfather hated flying in airplanes because he was not the sole person in control. I began to try to make myself aware that I, too, like my grandfather, was unnerved by things that were not in my control.
>
> I mentioned to my cooperating teacher that I was worried about being overly control conscious. He told me you have to walk a fine line between letting go and keeping the class in a positive structure. . . . My class had its own rhythm. Other classes I observed seemed to come to order sooner. My class, on the other hand, usually needed 5 minutes to settle in. Once I realized this I tuned into their pattern and chalked up the first few minutes to explaining what I wanted them to write for the WRITE NOW.
>
> I realize now that a lesson plan is only a blueprint for a class period. The key word for a good lesson seems to be . . . spontaneity. One student teacher told the class about how she used the developmental lesson plan exclusive of the students. Her cooperating teacher pointed out to her that she was not listening to what the students had answered. She was preoccupied with going down her list of questions. She realized she could have spun the lesson from one answer and opened up the class for a discussion and still accomplished her instructional objectives. Her honest admission made a big impression on me because I realized I was often making the same mistake. Again, I thought of the need for control. Now I see as a teacher the need to lose control constructively, or instructionally.

Here we see a student teacher scrutinizing his own character in order to understand his behavior in the classroom. His concern is with teaching better lessons, but he understands that his behavior cannot be seen only in terms of such pedagogical prescriptions as might be derived from the studies on wait time. The way we behave in classrooms reflects deep-seated aspects of our nature. We have here an example of a habit of self-scrutiny, and a willingness to alter classroom behavior as a result of self-understanding.

The student teacher then refers to comments made by a young woman, another student teacher, in a teacher training seminar. She reported on a lesson she had taught while being observed by a college supervisor. She had prepared a set of questions about a piece of literature and had focused on moving through them. In doing so, she had lost sight of the responses of the students and of the possibilities these presented for extended discussion of the work. The student teacher writing the essay recognizes the similarities to his own classroom behavior in the report of his colleague. He is impressed by her honesty. He recognizes something going on here besides the simple accumulation of knowledge. She has seen the need to give up a pattern of behavior that has served certain of her purposes, and to embrace another because the first pattern is getting in the way of student learning and of her becoming a better teacher. Her capacity for self-perception is what we are talking about when we use the term *flexibility*. It serves us well in all areas of life, and most certainly in our teaching. She helps not only herself but the writer of the essay. He is given strength when he learns there is someone else out there with the same problems he has, and with the courage to face up to them.

Applications of questioning techniques are enhanced by an understanding of the young people with whom the teacher is dealing, and by a general knowledge and keen perception of the world. Teachers responding to student answers are advised to be sensitive to the impact of their comments on students. There is concern that critical teacher comments will do long-term damage to students' willingness to participate in class discussions. Category systems are devised in which teacher comments on student answers are classified as positive and negative. Teachers are cautioned to avoid negative responses to students. Much of this makes sense and is certainly preferable to insensitivity.

However, flexibility and wisdom in individual application are also called for. Stock responses, aimed at making students feel good but ignoring the context of the discussion under way in class, are likely to be perceived as patronizing by those to whom they are offered in the hope of avoiding offense or psychological damage. ("That's very interesting. And what do *you* think, Charles?") Here again, methods of questioning can not be reduced to formulas and prescriptions. One student, at a given moment in his development, may need a great deal of overt encouragement in order to participate; another may see critical give-and-take with the teacher as a sign of psychological acceptance. Different climates for discussion may be required in different classes.

There is the inevitable need for wise judgments based on an understanding of the individuals with whom the teacher is dealing and the particular educational situation in which the interaction is occurring.

Intelligent teacher questioning requires not only an effort to understand individual students but a broader understanding of the world. A student teacher I supervised was using a novel about India in her tenth-grade English class. There was a pupil from India in the class, and I was disappointed that the teacher did not draw her into a particular discussion that turned on language, objects, and practices peculiar to India. When I raised this issue with the teacher in our after-class discussion, she pointed out that she had often been embarrassed and upset when, as the only African American in a college English class, she was called on to comment on some aspect of a piece of literature by a black author. She told me she knew the Indian student in her class quite well and had decided that the student would be unhappy if singled out to answer questions about Indian culture. Perhaps she would provide the student with an opportunity to discuss her experiences in India in relation to the novel, in an essay to be assigned. On the other hand, the student teacher assured me, there was an Indian student in another class who loved to talk about her native land to the other students in the class. As they read the novel in that class, she would be sure to call on her. These are the sorts of judgments a teacher must make. One can be aware of questioning techniques and of generalizations about multicultural sensitivity, but no classroom formulas can substitute for the wise, informed judgments of teachers, rooted in their own liberal education and reflective experience of the world.

I have listened to teachers questioning students about *Ethan Frome* or *Macbeth*. Is it any wonder that those teachers who have reflected long and hard on the complexities of love and marriage, ambition and manipulation, can ask wiser questions about the works under consideration, questions that will lead students to come to grips with these issues in their own lives? The depth of understanding they bring to such issues is also reflected in the sort of questions social studies or science teachers formulate for their students.

The asking of questions, then, like much else that goes on in classrooms, is affected by more than just technical knowledge. Question-asking is a complex enterprise. A technology of question-asking using a levels-of-questioning approach derived from Bloom's taxonomy of educational objectives, or the concepts of wait time and convergent and divergent questions, can be quite useful. Techniques such as these need to be enriched, however, by broader understandings of self, subject matter, and the world around us. Such broader understandings need to be linked to teaching practice. Methods courses and approaches to student teaching should be suffused with the spirit of a liberal education.

JOHN DEWEY AND THE PROBLEM OF METHODS

The language of teaching methods too often escapes from its context (the matter being taught and the purposes of the teacher and learner). Our use of concepts such as "motivation" and "discipline" leads us to make separate things of them, as in the sentences: "What is the motivation of your lesson?" and "No matter how much you know about your subject, you won't be able to teach until you establish some discipline in your class." Thus, motivation and discipline become something to be added to the already formulated lesson.

The notion that the enterprise of teacher education should focus on methods and practice, *apart* from questions of content and purpose, institutionalizes the original conceptual error and damages the possibilities of creating a useful education for teachers. Professional teacher education is assigned to handle one side of a misleading distinction. Insofar as it accepts this assignment without some reformulation of the assumptions underpinning it, it dooms itself to failure.

John Dewey (1964) tried to overcome this matter/methods dichotomy. His educational theory was itself part of an extraordinarily systematic and consistent set of broader philosophical understandings. Everywhere, Dewey sought to move beyond what he saw as limiting conceptual dichotomies to which the matter/methods one is related: mind/body; labor/leisure; subject/object. In his reformulation of the matter/methods dichotomy, he offered helpful ways of looking at the issue of teaching methods, implying in his writings that teacher education cannot be isolated from the subject being taught or from questions of educational purpose. At the same time, however, Dewey's formulation of the interaction of matter and methods places enormous burdens on the teacher.

His basic category was "experience," and his question was how to make the child's experience educative. To be educative, for Dewey, an experience had to meet certain criteria.

> Thinking is the method of an educative experience. The essentials of method are therefore identical with the essentials of reflection. They are first that the pupil have a genuine situation of experience — that there be a continuous activity in which the child is interested for its own sake; secondly, that a genuine problem develop within this situation as a stimulus

to thought; third, that he possess the information and make the observations needed to deal with it; fourth, that suggested solutions occur to him, which he shall be responsible for developing in an orderly way; fifth, that he have opportunity and occasion to test his ideas by application, to make their meaning clear, and to discover for himself their validity. (1964, p. 163)

Dewey placed his learning theory inside his evolutionary understanding of the life and growth of organisms. He objected to what he saw as the "formalism" of classrooms, textbooks, and schools, which had ripped the funded knowledge of the human race from its roots in the efforts of human beings to survive and prosper within their environment. The schools' organization of knowledge had clouded its evolutionary usefulness and had transformed it into useless school stuff. The task of the new educators was not just to throw the students back upon raw experience, although Dewey saw a place for the raw and muddled in the educational process; some experiences, he pointed out, could overwhelm or bore the learner. The educator's task was to organize the experience so that it would be educative. For Dewey, the "motivation" and the "discipline" of the lesson would be built into the experience.

One did not begin with "learning," but with "doing." Children were to be set a task, a social task, a task that grew out of the social life of the school/community. They would be motivated and guided by an end in view, a purpose, not by some motivational technique extraneous to the task. Discipline would not be imposed from the outside but would emerge in attention to the details, to the craft necessary to accomplish the task. If the conditions of the task were structured properly by the teacher, the doer-learner's experience would be educative. Dewey contrasted this approach with what he saw as the artificiality of lessons learned and recited in the classroom. Learning would occur as children went about doing social tasks that they perceived as connected to their own life experience. The tasks, at first, were to be extensions of home life. Hence the gardens, shops, and kitchens that Dewey set up in a revolt against the formalism and artificiality of school subjects, and in an effort to recreate the community of an earlier age in which life's occupations had been more visible and accessible to young people.

Thus, Dewey's (1964) first specification for an educative experience is "that the pupil have a genuine situation of experience — that there be a continuous activity in which he is interested for its own sake . . . " (p. 163). The teacher is not to leap atop the desk, lampshade on head, to attract the student's attention to what otherwise might be dull and uninteresting subject matter. Interest is to be expected when the artificial arrangement of subject matter is abandoned for an arrangement that recreates the life of the society, that presents to the students real problems requiring solutions. "The genuine situation of experience" is the starting point. The child is not to be presented with some piece of knowledge that may possibly be useful in the future, but with a problem whose solution will require reflective activities.

When Dewey talks of teaching methods, he always moves the spotlight quickly from the teacher to the learner. His interest is in the question: Under what conditions do people learn effective ways of handling their world? The question for the teacher becomes: How can I structure the experience of the learner so that it will be genuinely reflective? The great pedagogical task is to reconnect inert information to the lives of students. Now that is an extraordinarily tall order for teachers. It is also an issue that has widened the rift between teacher educators and their colleagues in the liberal arts. To oversimplify the situation: Teachers in the liberal arts and sciences have tended to value the ways in which subject areas are organized, apart from the present experience and perceived problems of students; teacher educators, on the other hand, have championed Dewey's notion of recasting the subject matter in terms of the experiences and problems of the learner. Practicing teachers are torn between the horns of this dilemma.

Let us look for a moment at an effort to apply Dewey's understanding of methods, his organic concepts of interest and motivation and discipline. Very early in my teaching career, when I introduced the topic of prepositional phrases to my seventh-grade English class, a student asked me what good this—and, indeed, the learning of any grammar—would do him. Now, all teachers have been faced with questions like this. They often try to answer them directly. Sometimes they alter the way in which they teach a topic or a whole subject in an effort to make their purposes clear. Sometimes, as a result of such persistent questions, professional educators are moved as a group to debate the way in which a subject is taught, as English teachers have been by my student's question about grammar.

Dewey, and some of his followers who founded progressive schools, responded not merely by altering a lesson but by changing the workings of the whole school and its curriculum (Mayhew & Edwards, 1936). Dewey left the door open for piecemeal improvements by individual teachers, and many have tried to transform the inert materials of texts in the area they are teaching into usable knowledge for the work of children in classrooms.

I tried to adapt my sense of Dewey's thinking about teaching and learning to my seventh-grade English class. The lesson for the day could no longer be defined as adverbial phrases. That was the inert piece of knowledge Dewey so roundly condemned. I had to begin somewhere else. I was, and still am, convinced that the learning of grammar, among other things, is instrumental to good writing, and that good writing is not only a valuable asset in life in our society but a crucial tool in learning to think clearly.

Following Dewey, I needed to set up situations, preferably social ones, for my students, in which they could see the need to write and to write well. I had heard several pupils complaining that they would not be picked up by a school bus in the next year if planned budget cuts went through. So I decided to encourage the students to write to local school board members and to state officials. I was trying to satisfy Dewey's (1964) first and second criteria for an educative experience — that it be "a genuine situation of experience — that there be a continuous situation in which he [the learner] is interested for its own sake," and "that a genuine problem develop within this situation as a stimulus to thought" (p. 163). Some, not all, of the students were interested in the transportation problem, and, of the group interested in the issue, only some were interested in writing to officials as a channel for their interests. I had then to find out from the rest what they *were* interested in, and who an audience for their writing might be. My classroom organization grew more difficult.

Dewey's third criterion is that the learners "possess the information and make the observations needed to deal with it" (p. 163). Working at first only with the group that had chosen to write to officials about the bus transportation problem, I steered them, on the one hand, to information about taxes, about practices in neighboring school districts, about pedestrian accidents, and, on the other hand, as they composed their letters, to information about how to write effectively. This included grammatical errors I noticed in their first drafts, such as ending a sentence in a preposition or mistaking sentence fragments for sentences. I also focused on ways of developing an argument and on considerations of tone and how it affected one's audience. When I began identifying grammatical errors and started to work on correcting them (adverbial phrases were not even in the running for my attention), I ran head-on into another major problem with Dewey's alternative to the artificial and inert organization of subject matter. He wanted me to avoid, in this case, trying to teach grammar in the order in which it had been organized in a text, unconnected to the experience and problems of these young people. He was right. Most of the students were not interested in adverbial phrases. But now, as I corrected my students' writing errors and tried to explain concepts such as the agreement of subject and verb or what makes a sentence a sentence, I found myself thinking that it might be helpful to have a carefully organized grammar text that would help the students to develop a language about their own writing—that is, a grammar. In order to help them solve their problems involved in writing an effective letter to local representatives on an issue that interested them, I considered adopting a formal text. But if I went back to such a grammar text, I would begin to put distance between a body of knowledge and the experiences and perceived problems of my students.

"Don't retreat from the Deweyan perspective," say the teacher educators. "See, we told you so," say my colleagues in the liberal arts. "We have been a long time in formulating the knowledge of grammar in a logical and orderly fashion. Your students will just have to be patient and learn the grammar in a logical fashion. Then they will be better equipped to handle whatever problems they have in the future that require competent writing."

Perhaps a compromise is in order. We need to go back and forth between the Deweyan ideal of experience rooted in the perceived problems of the learner, and an effort to develop concepts with students even when they do not see an immediate application of these concepts to their present experience. We might benefit from the heretical recognition that the fundamental ideal of democratic education—interesting all students in all subjects every day—may take a terrible toll on disappointed teachers. The ideal might be modified with the realistic recognition that not every student will be interested in every subject even when it is placed in the context of present experience and problems. No one is interested in all of life's experiences and problems. Some, unfortunately, are interested in very few. Providing some sort of context for any study, as in the example of grammar, certainly makes sense, but it is hardly a guarantee of interest. Nor will every student need constant reminders of connections to life problems. Some move forward out of a love for the intricacies of language or number that seems to outstrip present tasks to be accomplished. Dewey is right to urge us to discard external notions of motivation, interest, and discipline, and to locate each within the learning experience itself. At the same time, there would seem to be an art in choosing when to emphasize the connections of a subject to the life experiences of students and when to focus on other motivations.

Teachers learning how to teach thus become enmeshed in fundamental philosophical differences over educational purpose and practice. They must address these issues not as abstract ideologies but as guiding principles for classroom practice. Their work in the classroom provides a marvelous opportunity for the illustration of the remaining two criteria for Dewey's educational experience: "that suggested solutions occur to him, which he shall be responsible for developing in an orderly way; fifth, that he have opportunity and occasion to test his ideas by application, to make their meaning clear, and to discover for himself their validity" (1964, p. 163). The teacher's own experience must be educative, reflective, and wisely tested in the classroom.

7

ONLY TWO CHEERS FOR
TEACHING AS A PROFESSION

Teachers are encouraged by educational researchers and teacher educators to don the mantle of professionalism today for the same reasons
that social climbers were urged to don a Chesterfield coat in the early
days of this century. Much writing about teaching or teacher education
either insists that teaching is a profession or sketches out ways in which
it might become one.

The word "professional," as applied to teaching, has undergone a
positive revival in the last decade. It has been used as an honorific even
by teacher union leaders with a realistic grasp of power relations in
the schools and the larger society (Shanker, 1985). Teachers, teacher
educators, and educational reformers have embraced the notion of professionalism. In doing so, Linda Darling-Hammond (1988) points out,
they have raised suspicions:

> Misinterpreting professionalization as mainly a quest for money, status,
> and autonomy, opponents worry that "empowered" teachers will be unac-
> countable. They fail to understand that the major reason for seeking to
> create a profession of teaching is that it will increase the probability that
> all students will be well educated because they are well taught—that
> professionalism seeks to heighten accountability by investing in knowledge
> and its responsible use. (p. 8)

I want to suggest, counter to Darling-Hammond's argument, that
even a sympathetic analysis of the rhetoric used in reports and studies
on teacher education published in the last decade reveals a central
concern with status and with the income and autonomy related to it.
At the same time, one can also acknowledge in the focus on professionalism a concern with providing structures and guidelines (such as more
demanding teacher certification procedures, more involvement of teachers in school decision-making) that, in the long run, will improve the
education of young people in schools.

Here is an abstract and truncated version of the argument for a teaching profession: Teaching requires complex knowledge and skill. Those who go through a long and difficult course of study at the college or university level acquire this knowledge and skill and should, therefore, be trusted to make decisions about curriculum, school organization, teaching methods, and other aspects of education. Teachers will set up a professional practices board at the state or national level to ascertain through testing and other means whether those seeking entry to the profession have acquired the necessary knowledge, and whether those seeking promotion within the profession have attained a level of ability warranting it. Teachers will use their knowledge in the interest of clients—that is, altruistically. The possession of knowledge disseminated in a university setting and originating from within a scientific mode of inquiry generates a public trust in the ability of teachers to make significant educational decisions. Intellectual and ethical norms are created and implemented within a collegium, a community of peers, at both local and national levels. Moreover, teachers given more responsibility for educational decision-making will find their work more rewarding. Everyone involved will benefit.

A new social contract is struck. I am concerned, however, with the ways in which certain concepts within the argument are construed by various groups, and with the implications for teaching practice that flow from those constructs. How we understand the key concepts of "knowledge," "altruism," and "collegium" will affect not only the way in which we organize schools but, more importantly, the way in which we educate teachers and the ways in which teachers think and act in schools.

KNOWLEDGE

The claim to a specialized knowledge is an important part of the argument for the development of a teaching profession. David Berliner (1987), in discussing the old question of the extent to which teaching is an art or a science, points out that medicine, too, is an art but "that without its close ties to science it would be without success, status and power in our society" (p. 4). Doctors, he tells us,

> have become wealthy and respected . . . because they have acquired knowledge, skills, concepts, and technology. . . . I firmly believe that now it is our turn. We now have something that an ordinary person does not have—a knowledge base consisting of facts, concepts and technology that can transform our profession as well. . . . The transformation we envision will put us on a scientific and technological track that will com-

mand the public's faith in and admiration of our competence. I believe we will get their full support when they believe that our services cannot be performed by ordinary, untrained, inexperienced members of society. (p. 5)

Berliner emphasizes the discontinuity between the knowledge of the teacher and that of the ordinary member of society. The remainder of his article – the bulk of it – consists of a series of detailed arguments defending the quality and reliability of educational research in relation to research in other areas, including chemistry and physics, and the usefulness of that research to classroom teachers. He concludes his piece by asserting that knowledge and skill gave to the legal and the medical professions the high status they now hold. "Knowledge is clearly power, a kind of social power. It commands respect and confers status in our technologically oriented society. . . . Educational research is fully prepared to bring that kind of power to the teaching profession" (p. 5).

From the Baconian notion of knowledge as power to transform the environment, we have moved to a notion of knowledge as power to command respect and confer status. It is difficult to misinterpret Berliner's concerns. His article and the rest of the articles in the book to which it is an introduction are addressed to classroom teachers. He argues for the connection between the possession of knowledge and skills, and the status and financial well-being of the teacher. The rest of the book, consisting of reports on major areas of educational research, strikes me as both formidable and quite useful to teachers. Such recent research on teaching, and its dissemination in college- and university-based teacher education courses, will surely play an important part in changes in the teaching profession, and generally in the reform agenda for schools. But arguments emanating from the university research community are likely to overstate the case for the significance of a scientifically grounded knowledge base as the key to effective teaching and to increased status and income for members of the teaching profession.

The Holmes Group (its original governing board consisted of 14 deans from leading graduate schools of education), in its influential report (1986), offered differential staffing as an important part of the reform of the teaching profession and of teacher education. The authors of the report pointed out the benefits of the concept to various groups, including, to their credit, the benefits to their own institutions:

Improved teacher education must accompany and be accompanied by changes in the role, function, and nature of teaching. . . . To create a market for professionally trained teachers with advanced graduate credentials, it is essential to provide expanded career opportunities and rewards in teaching. Otherwise prospective teachers will have few incentives to invest in the demanding professional education essential to competent teaching. (pp. 40–41)

Teaching seems so clearly different from the specialized occupations (such as medicine) to which it is often compared, that one has to wonder whether the notion of the acquisition of a specialized knowledge base is as central to what it means to become a competent teacher as the educational researchers argue. The understandable self-interest of graduate research teacher education institutions—and the equally understandable desire on the part of teachers to achieve prestige and public trust by associating the process of learning to teach with scientific endeavors, and by locating that learning in a university setting—may skew our inquiry into the sorts of knowledge and the kinds of preparation that teachers sorely need. In putting the cart before the horse, in focusing on questions of status and public trust rather than on what sort of knowledge is most useful to teachers and under what conditions it might best be acquired, we choose the wrong road.

One is more likely to get a thoughtful discussion about the sort of knowledge needed by teachers, and the kind of education most likely to contribute to it, from someone not giving questions of professional prestige and reward prominence in the inquiry. The British philosopher of education, John Wilson (1979), who spends a great deal of his time talking to beginning teachers, is one such inquirer. He argues that while some knowledge of theory and research is likely to prove useful, while competence and skills gained through practical training are clearly necessary, and while fundamental character traits in some people contribute to their teaching ability, none of these gets at the heart of the matter.

Good teachers, he tells us,

> are keen on their subject and have a strong desire that others should be keen also; they understand and care for their pupils; they are not afraid to maintain discipline; they are tolerably sane and secure people; they have a sense of humour; and they are not crippled by doctrinaire fantasies about education. These qualities are mostly a matter of attitude, not of skills at all. (p. 86)

Attitudes, for Wilson, are composed of beliefs, feelings, and tendencies to act in certain ways. The beliefs can be discussed philosophically; the feelings, and the reasons underlying the feelings, can be evoked and inspected; and the actions of teachers in classrooms and schools can be observed and examined. The teacher's education might take a variety of forms, including reading, lectures, role-playing, and reflective experiences. There is a manageable set of topics and issues that need to be addressed (for example, questions of authority in the classroom, of race, of attitudes toward the subject one teaches). Where muddled thinking exists on these issues we need to move toward reflective analysis.

This sort of teacher education, Wilson tells us, can best be carried out with working groups of students and faculty who can build up the kind of trust and understanding necessary for the enterprise. Wilson is aware that his Socratic notion of the sort of knowledge needed in teacher education, a kind of self-examination and an examination of the broader contexts within which teachers work, will not strike the educational bureaucrats as particularly appealing. It is much too sensible, modest, and vague. It lacks the promise of an educational science diagnosing the problems of students and offering them prescriptions, and the prestige of an emphasis on a university-based scholarship. It points away from an education for teachers centered on a scientifically generated knowledge base and toward a rather old-fashioned notion of knowledge as a painful questioning of our own beliefs and attitudes, a personal growth attained through an examination of our own actions in the public world. It is a notion arrived at, not out of concern with teacher prestige or the growth of graduate institutions, but simply by focusing on the questions of what sorts of qualities we value in teachers and how we can create educational situations in which those qualities are likely to develop. The horse is back in front of the cart.

It is ironic that Berliner and others have chosen to bet on a scientific research base as the key to an improved teacher education, and to the development of a specialized profession that will gain the trust and admiration of the public, just when the modeling of social science on oversimplified understandings of what physical scientists are doing is being called into question (Manicas, 1987). At a time when the doors of the university have opened to a variety of research methods into human behavior, the educational researchers focusing on teacher effectiveness have reached a point where much of their work is at last conceptually sophisticated, rigorously executed, and relevant to classroom practice. Just as the curtain is about to go up, the audience is leaving for new forms of theater being offered in the neighborhood.

The argument developed by Donald Schön, for example, on the nature of how practitioners think in the various professions has received a particularly sympathetic reception among many teacher educators (Schön, 1983, 1987; Grimmett & Erickson, 1988). Looking at professionals as varied as town planners, therapists, and teachers, Schön claims that the situations of complexity, uncertainty, instability, uniqueness, and value conflict in which they find themselves do not fit with the epistemology of technical rationality that reigns in the university-based professional programs. The expectation that the problems of the professional practitioner will be solved through the application of techniques derived as rules from a scientific study of how things work simply doesn't hold up in the complex mess of daily goings-on. Schön chooses to examine what he calls an epistemology of reflective practice, implicit in professionals' artful negotiating of their daily work. He is interested in practitioners' efforts to explain what they are doing and why they are doing it. His focus is on the sort of knowledge that is not a generalization applied to practice but a concrete response embedded in and discoverable through an examination of practice.

In thinking about the relationship between knowledge and the profession of teaching, we need to look also at the connection between general and specialized knowledge. Professionals are supposed to be generally learned, as well as expert in their own work. In the preparation of teachers, the general education can be seen as continuous with professional preparation in ways that would not be true of the connection between a general education and the professional preparation of doctors. Firstly, and most obviously, the content of the general education (for example, a course in American history or in geology) serves as the basis of knowledge for the teacher, who may be called on to teach such subjects at the elementary or secondary level. All the reformers agree that there is a need to strengthen the general education component of the teacher's preparation. Some, such as the authors of the Holmes report (Holmes Group, 1986), go on to urge specific changes in our approach to general education. They insist that no teachers should be allowed to teach subjects they have not studied deeply, that undergraduate general education courses should be taught by faculty members, who "understand the pedagogy of their material"; and that the courses should be organized "so that undergraduate students can gain a sense of the intellectual structure and boundaries of their disciplines, rather than taking a series of disjointed, prematurely specialized fragments" (p. 17).

A second reason for the importance of a general education for teachers is suggested by John Wilson's (1979) argument about the sorts of qualities needed by good teachers; it turns out that these qualities are also found in good parents, in good counselors — and in good people. And the Socratic questioning of the self and of one's place in the world that Wilson describes as central to the education of teachers is precisely the sort of project in which the best teachers and students in general education courses have always been engaged. If we accept Wilson's notion of the purpose and practice of teacher education, and I do, then the general education and professional education components of a teacher's education are continuous in a strong sense. Professional knowledge, in this view, consists of a deepening and focusing of the general knowledge available to all, rather than a specialized expert knowledge inaccessible to, in Berliner's earlier-cited phrase, "ordinary, untrained, inexperienced members of society" (p. 86).

ALTRUISM

Recall the general argument for teacher professionalism: If teachers possess a specialized knowledge base, they can be allowed to make significant educational decisions. But we also want to know that their decision-making will be based not on self-interest but on altruism. In answering the question of what it means to be a professional, Albert Shanker (1985) lists four characteristics: high standards of entry, a knowledge base, collegial relationships in which professionals act in accordance with what peers expect of them on the basis of their knowledge, and an intent to act in the interest of clients. Shanker points out — correctly, I believe — that the pendulum has swung from a time when powerless teachers were patted on the head on Teacher Recognition Day. "We tend to be viewed today as though we are acting only in our self-interest. . . . That image is standing in the way of our professional status. We must act on behalf of our clients and be perceived as acting that way" (p. 5).

Arguments for the recognition of any group as a profession run the risk of being dismissed as self-serving propaganda designed to enhance the power, status, and financial rewards of the group in question. Society is better off, nevertheless, for having professions that make an effort to create among their membership a sense that action toward ends other than those of self-interest is a significant part of what it means to be a member of the group. One need not be naive to recognize that many doctors have made extraordinary, even heroic, sacrifices of time and energy for the benefit of their patients; others, of course, have not allowed the interests of patients to interfere with their own greed. Such moments of sacrifice are indeed a part of the social definition of what it is to be a doctor. In fact, assertions of professional altruism can serve either as a smokescreen for greed or as a context of expectation for truly admirable behavior.

Teaching, like medicine, and unlike advertising, seems to have built into it an altruistic purpose. The physician is there to make you well, the advertiser to convince you to buy a product or service, and the teacher to help you learn. We consider both health and genuine learning, as opposed to indoctrination, desirable. Products or services may or may not be desirable. When it comes to altruism, teachers have a leg up on many others in the society. They are not, after all, selling mayonnaise. Oddly, teacher education reports make very little of the altruistic presumption inherent in the work of teachers; they emphasize, instead, plans for new career patterns and dramatic income increases as ways to recruit competent teachers. Oddly, too, the recent reports and commentaries spend little time analyzing just what forms teacher altruism might take and what such different forms might mean for everyday teaching practice.

If we are to argue that altruism is a central component of what it means to be a member of the teaching profession, we need to look at what forms that altruism might take, and what effect such forms might have on the education of teachers and on their daily practice in schools. The Carnegie report (Carnegie Forum on Education and the Economy, 1986), for example, emphasized the relationship between education and the changing nature of world economic competition:

> If America wants to compete on the same terms as it did in the past— making the most of workers with low skill levels—then it must accept prevailing world wage levels for low-skilled and semi-skilled labor. That is, we must be prepared for a massive decline in our standard of living. The alternative is to revise our view of the role of the worker in the economy. In the future, high wage level societies will be those whose economies are based on the use on a wide scale of very highly skilled workers, backed up by the most advanced technologies available. (p. 3)

From there the argument is simple. The educational system must be rebuilt to meet the challenge of international economic competition. Teachers will be a crucial part of the rebuilt educational system, and we must, as a society, make sure that qualified people are attracted to teaching. Even if we could remain competitive without rebuilding our educational system, the Carnegie authors tell us, there are other compelling reasons for doing so—for example, providing equal opportunity for all children and preserving an informed population capable of self-government.

Teacher altruism is, then, tied to educational purpose. And purposes vary, requiring continuing inquiry and adjustment. How shall we define the good that we are doing, and what forms shall our teaching preparation and practice take as a result of our definition? Teachers' altruism, what it is exactly that we are doing for others, is not a given. Nor can we sit down and settle its form in a once-and-for-all fashion, and deduce from it an appropriate teacher education and a way to carry on one's teaching practice.

The same teaching practice can obviously serve more than one end; it is a distortion of means–ends discussions to assume that widespread activities are going on with all participants agreeing on or even conscious of a single outcome. Further, schools operate within larger contexts that tend to define their functions in society regardless of the teachers' intentions. Thus, many teachers see themselves as engaged primarily in encouraging critical thinking in their students, while the societal message about schools is that they are there to enhance social and economic mobility, or at least protect against a downward slide.

Teacher altruism emerges, then, as far more than a matter of public relations. For purpose is at the heart of the educational enterprise, and inquiry into that purpose must be placed at the heart of teacher education and of the teacher's daily practice. Granted, we wish to do good for our students and for society, but exactly what forms will that activity take? I am not speaking here of the professional expertise for which Berliner and others argue, for the accumulation of a knowledge base that teacher experts can apply in appropriate situations. Plato confused such expertise with moral inquiry a long time ago. He argued that the leaders of a society are like doctors or navigators. If one wishes to achieve health, one does not do as one pleases, but consults the doctor with specialized knowledge. If they wish to reach their destination safely, the sailors ought not to fight among themselves for control of the ship but consult the navigator, who appears to be wasting his time gazing at the stars, but in fact knows how to guide the ship to port. Plato argued for a professional leadership class that would be subjected to a long course of study, tested at various points along the way, and finally allowed to rule. But unlike doctors and navigators, whose ends were fairly well defined and who were expected above all to acquire and demonstrate an instrumental body of knowledge, Plato's leaders and our teachers are faced with the task of defining ends or purposes as they go about their business; familiarity with a pedagogical knowledge base is not the prime requisite for this task.

Teachers choose to act altruistically or otherwise in a variety of concrete situations. It is difficult, in these situations, to untangle the instrumental from questions of educational ends. A teacher speaks to a child about the child's apparent lack of interest. The content of their discussion may be shaped partly by the teacher's previous reflection on the nature of his larger purposes in educating young people and on his practical judgment about the directions in which this particular young person is moving. Reflective teachers discover the forms their altruism is taking as they move along; ponder their actions; alter them in the light of their reflections; and recognize that these forms are multiple and concrete. A teacher's education should include opportunities to discuss concrete interactions with students, large- and small-scale curriculum choices, and a variety of other ongoing activities in relation to the forms that altruism might take. What mixture of concern with young peoples' future careers, personal growth, roles as citizens, and critical capacities or with the nation's economic well-being should enter into teachers' choices about what is to be taught and how it is to be taught? The ethical concerns that are part and parcel of the teacher's work constitute an argument against a teacher education construed as primarily scientific, instrumental, and specialized.

COLLEGIUM

The argument for a teaching profession asserts that teachers should be given more responsibility in the workplace because of their specialized knowledge and altruism. In turn, those who would reform the teaching profession argue that such responsible work will be more attractive to beginners and more satisfying to those already in the profession. Thus, various reform documents urge a restructuring of the workplace and a reorganization of the profession itself. Unfortunately, although the reformers started off talking about a collegium — a community of peers developing policy within schools — they wound up with a hierarchy that appears to negate the benefits offered by the collegium.

The Holmes report (1986) urged that "we make and reward formal distinctions about responsibilities and degrees of autonomy" (p. 39) and called for a form of differentiated staffing: "It would be possible to limit the autonomy of certain teachers who would work under various degrees of supervision, thereby avoiding the traditional practice of bestowing full professional prerogatives on everyone brought into the classroom, regardless of their credentials or demonstrated abilities" (p. 40). The differentiated profession would be divided into three groups: instructors, professional teachers, and career professional teachers. Instructors would be capable college graduates not making a career commitment to teaching; their lessons would be structured and reviewed by qualified professional teachers. The instructors would have no policy, curriculum, or guidance responsibilities. Professional teachers, the second group in the hierarchy, would have full autonomy in their own classrooms. Their knowledge about children would allow them to decide, when necessary, whether to seek outside help or handle problems themselves; they would participate with experts such as child psychologists in making decisions about children's futures; and they would be child advocates, ensuring that their communities and schools met the educational needs of students. The third group, career professional teachers, would be involved in such specialized roles as teacher education, curriculum improvement, working with parents, and conducting research. In the Holmes Group's view, these career professional teachers would constitute 20 percent of the teaching force.

The authors of the report say that their notion of differentiated staffing will benefit three groups: teachers, teacher educators, and the public schools. Individual teachers will go on to more fulfilling and higher-paid work within the course of their teaching careers. Teachers in general will play a vital role in creating better schools. Teacher educators will benefit because teachers, knowing they will be rewarded for specialized work, will invest in graduate education. The public schools will benefit because in a teacher shortage they will be able to staff classrooms without permanently credentialing teachers. The instructor group is thus meant "to respond to disequilibrium in the supply of and demand for teachers. . . . The concept of differentiated staffing would permit responsible expansion and contraction of a pool of teachers, while protecting the integrity of the professional teaching force" (1986, pp. 39–40).

The Carnegie report (1986) also called for a form of differentiated staffing within the context of a concern with the professional autonomy of teachers. The Holmes Group's career professional teacher is the Carnegie Forum's lead teacher. Lead teachers would be expected to create, not another bureaucracy, but a school community. "They would take collective responsibility for helping colleagues who were not performing up to par by arranging for coaching, technical assistance, coursework or other remediation that might be called for" (p. 3).

Albert Shanker (1985), in addressing issues of teacher autonomy and collegial responsibility, ended, like the authors of the Holmes and Carnegie reports, by championing the notion of differentiated staffing. He began with the argument for responsibility warranted by expertise. "A professional is a person who is an expert and, by virtue of his or her expertise, is permitted to operate fairly independently, to make decisions, to exercise discretion, to be free of most direct supervision" (p. 6). Shanker sees a higher degree of teacher autonomy as consonant with changes in American work styles. Americans, he tells us, no longer view work as only a necessary means of earning income. They now look to their jobs for satisfaction, respect, and a sense of their own worth. At work, they enjoy being called on to exercise their own judgment. Shanker observes that "our schools are the last bastions of the rigid 19th-century industrial hierarchy" (p. 7). He sees teachers, even in some of the new reform proposals, still being told what textbooks to use and how many hours to teach each subject, still not trusted by those in power to make professional decisions. He argues that both the person and the enterprise benefit when individuals are given some control over their work environment.

Wary that the differentiated staffing proposals are merely disguised merit pay policies, Shanker nevertheless embraces them. He talks about senior teachers conducting internships for new teachers. These teachers might also be evaluating textbooks, creating curricula, and teaching courses in curriculum-making and textbook evaluation to others. They would receive appointments at the local university and higher pay for their work. They would bring a needed dimension to the education of teachers. To his credit, Shanker states bluntly the reasons why the delivery of educational services must be restructured: demographics and economics. He reminds us that half of the 2 million teachers in the country will be retired over the next decade. Given the demand for talent in private industries and government agencies public education will have a difficult time attracting career teachers. He argues that we cannot afford the money needed to recruit and retain a sufficient number of qualified teachers.

The answer for Shanker, as for the authors of the other reports, is to have a much smaller number of career teachers, "perhaps only a third as many" (p. 23), who would be paid high salaries indeed. Technology in the form of educational videocassettes would replace the portion of teachers' time — too much of it, according to the most thoughtful and sympathetic critics — that is presently spent in lecturing. And there would be a group of "idealistic transients, . . . who did not intend to stay more than five years or so" (p. 21) working under the mentorship of the career teachers. Career teachers would engage in "coaching students, teaching thinking skills, stimulating creativity, . . . helping students learn to reason, argue and persuade" (p. 22).

We have another cart and horse problem here. Differentiated staffing has been recommended as a solution to the claimed teacher shortage problem; we provide status, increased responsibility, and higher income for some in order to attract more and better people into the profession. As we have seen, differentiated staffing is also helpful to school boards looking to create a large group of untenurable people who can be easily hired and dismissed as the student population rises and falls. It is also helpful to graduate schools of education seeking students in need of advanced certification. These goals are not necessarily objectionable. Were the horse before the cart, however, we would ask the question: How can we best arrange the workplace for teachers so they might carry on their task of encouraging student learning? Differentiated staffing would not be the answer.

The differentiated staffing notion as presented in various reports includes a large group of individuals teaching in classrooms—the instructors, or "transient idealists"—who do not share in the rewards of autonomous decision-making. There is a kind of double-speak quality in the discussions about this group. On the one hand, they are described as bright college graduates, idealistic Peace Corps types, who know their subject matter; on the other hand, we are told, they will have their plans reviewed by career teachers or senior teachers or lead teachers, and they will not be involved in textbook selection, curriculum planning, meeting with parents, or similar responsibilities. This is double-speak because the speakers are packaging the same concept differently for two different constituencies. To those concerned with financing teacher salaries, the instructors are offered as a class who will subsidize, through their lower salaries, significantly higher salaries for a smaller group of career teachers. They will have no certification, hence no tenure, and can be let go as school populations shift. At the same time, the reformers are trying to assure the public that this teaching underclass will be competent to work with their children. This is not unlike the decisions of some unions, when faced with a total money offer from management, to set one wage and benefits package for senior workers and another, less lucrative one for juniors. A similar arrangement is in the air here between those charged with the financing and management of schools and some teacher leaders. The larger public and the instructors or "transient idealists" have not been invited to the bargaining table.

Will the underclass of teachers really be happy if the concept of differentiated staffing is translated into widespread practice? Shanker's argument for self-fulfillment on the job makes sense and is, of course, equally applicable to all teachers. One senses that these hands-on classroom teachers, if they are worth their salt, will want to begin participating in selecting appropriate materials for their students, designing curricula, and meeting with parents. The complaint of teachers all along has been that such tasks ought to be done by those in the classrooms who know the students best, and not by distant administrators. Professional teachers basing their claims to expertise on advanced work in research-oriented graduate schools will not be perceived by the new teaching underclass as any more legitimate than today's administrators.

Hierarchical workplace arrangements run the risk of reducing the possibility that a school will become the site for a genuine teacher education. Maximizing open interaction within a community of teachers, all inquiring into a set of common tasks for which they share responsibility, seems a much more promising program for teacher education reform to follow.

I can muster only two cheers for the concept of teaching as a profession until we (1) reject the exclusive notion of teacher knowledge as a set of established, scientific truth claims, the too-often-proclaimed knowledge base, and (2) explore a broader vision of teacher knowledge, including efforts to bring broader perspectives to bear on school problems, to examine our own attitudes and actions in the light of their impact on student learning, and to reflect on the implications of good teaching practice. In this exploration of a broader vision of teacher education, we need also to ask where, with whom, and under what conditions various aspects of it might take place. None of these inquiries should be bounded by issues of teacher prestige.

I have only two cheers for teaching as a profession until the claims for teacher altruism are treated as something more than a calculated move to gain public support, and until we take seriously the notion that what is best for the young people we serve is not at all a given, and ought in fact to be part of the sort of inquiry in which teachers are engaged daily. I have only two cheers until we dissociate the call to professionalism from plans that separate teachers into groups in which only a few have access to appropriate responsibilities and rewards, and that negate the possibility of a community of teachers inquiring into and acting together on school policies.

There is a wistful quality to much of the recent literature examining teacher education and teacher professionalism. Concerns with the sense of status and self-worth of teachers and teacher educators seem more than just an effort to create a context in which better teachers will be attracted to the work (Goodlad, 1990). There is a deeply personal aspect to all of this. Teacher educators and researchers allow perceptions of other college and university faculty to undermine their own sense of the importance of the work they are doing themselves and the work for which they are preparing others. Too often, these misperceptions lead to wrongheaded thinking about the relation of teacher education to the rest of the university.

8

THE PLACE OF TEACHER EDUCATION IN THE UNIVERSITY

If one believes with Victor Cousin that as the teacher goes, so goes the school, then the preparation of teachers becomes a decisive element in the shaping of any school system. And inasmuch as men disagree on the ends and means of education, they will inevitably disagree on the preparation of teachers.
—Lawrence Cremin (quoted in Borrowman, 1965, p. vii)

What should be the place of the school of education in the college or university? This question has been asked since the nineteenth century, but it is being asked ever more insistently and under changed circumstances in our own day. Contemporary discussions of the issue, like those about teaching as a profession, often describe and sometimes exhibit deep seated concerns about status and identity. They also focus on the survival of schools of education. Harry Judge (1982), in a sentence that begins in understatement and ends in uncharacteristic bluntness, captures the anxiety and anger of the teacher educators: "It is no great fun to work at places that are constantly sniffed at and spat upon" (p. 5).

One important contemporary argument is that the School of Education has been seduced by the mentality of the graduate school. It has turned itself into a research institution emulating the scholarship of the other denizens of the graduate schools and accepting their norms. In "studying education" it has abandoned its more important task of preparing teachers for the nation's schools. B. Othanel Smith (1980) tells us that this is not a new problem: "At the very outset colleges of pedagogy were therefore torn between the desire to achieve academic respectability and the need to prepare students to perform effectively on the job" (p. 13).

The norms of the graduate school are seen as shaping professors of education who, in identifying with the graduate school ethos, distance themselves from — indeed, turn their backs on — the public schools. Teacher educators lose touch with the schools because, in pursuing research, they neglect their service functions, such as student teacher supervision and curriculum reform work. Further, the sort of research that is rewarded in the academic culture is different from the sort of knowledge useful to teachers. The educational researchers take their cues from the problems in the academic discipline of which they are a part, rather than from what the teachers worry about in schools and classrooms. The researchers become imperialistic and seek to make inquiries into and publish work about issues distant from schooling, thereby neglecting the problems of the schools. The graduate school researchers are quantitatively and/or empirically oriented (in imitation of the social sciences imitating the natural sciences), and the real problems of the schools, the ones with which teachers are concerned, do not yield themselves to these sorts of inquiries. Some of the commentators also point out that it has done teacher educators little good with the rest of the university community to conform to the latter's norms. Respect has not been forthcoming.

The solution offered is that the schools of education should turn away from the university culture and its norms, and toward the teaching profession, to gain a sense of purpose and prestige. They should focus, we are told, on educating teachers, and their research function should be directly related to that primary task. The current debate, formulated as a choice between a graduate school mentality and true teacher education, is an updated and altered version of arguments that continued from the early part of the nineteenth century until shortly after World War II, over the relationship between a liberal and a professional or technical approach in the education of teachers. Some of the same issues remain and new ones have been added.

The growth of the American high school at one end and the development of graduate education at the other have largely deprived liberal or general education of a formidable institutional presence. The graduate school ethos has clearly affected undergraduate general or liberal education, moving it toward more specialization and toward a forgetfulness about its own historical purposes. When we talk about the relationship between professional teacher education and preparation in the liberal arts, we need to recognize that approaches in liberal or general education have been significantly altered by the rise in influence of the graduate school. The norms of graduate education thus affect both the liberal and the professional education of teachers.

What is it about the graduate school mentality that bothers some teacher educators? Are there aspects of it that might be salvaged for the education of teachers? What elements of a liberal education should we preserve in the education of teachers? These questions need to be addressed against the background of Cremin's notion that our disagreements over how we prepare teachers are rooted in fundamental differences about the purposes of their work and the means to attain them. My fear is that the many legitimate complaints of my colleagues in professional teacher education, about those charged with the task of general education and those responsible for graduate education, may lead to a new and narrowing isolationism.

THE DEVELOPMENT OF PERSONS
AS THE END OF LIBERAL EDUCATION

Let us look again at the place of the notion of a liberal or general education in the current teacher education reform debate. Both critics outside teacher education and teacher educators themselves agree that students planning to become teachers should have a strong general education. There is some debate about whether this means that there ought to be no undergraduate major in education, or that the number of education courses ought to be reduced in order to make more room for subject matter courses, or that the education program should be purely a graduate professional sequence with a strong clinical component. Finally, there is some dispute over what courses in the liberal arts ought to replace the undergraduate education courses. What, for example, is an appropriate undergraduate major for students preparing to become elementary school teachers? What is an appropriate distribution of general education courses for students preparing to become elementary or secondary school teachers?

Some teacher educators are upset because they are losing their undergraduate majors and/or having their course offerings reduced, but many are calling for abandoning undergraduate professional preparation altogether and seeking the prestige, autonomy, singleness of purpose, and better-prepared students promised by a professional master's program. These arguments about credit allotment between professional and liberal arts courses, and the question of choosing between an undergraduate and graduate preparation for teachers, take our eyes off the more basic questions: What forms should liberal and professional elements in teacher education take, and how will each contribute to the creation of the sort of teacher we desire?

The disputes about the content of a liberal education articulate or assume two purposes for it: (1) the mastery of subject matter to be taught at the elementary or secondary level, and (2) preprofessional preparation—for example, the study of psychology as a preparation for more professionally oriented courses on learning and classroom management. I have been arguing all along that the connection between a general liberal education and the work of the teacher is stronger than the connection between a liberal education and the work of other professionals.

A liberal education has always been defended on the grounds that it developed the whole person; that is, it made carpenters persons rather than making persons carpenters. It allowed us to make wise judgments about significant matters. At various times, different subjects have been touted as enabling us to think more effectively and wisely: grammar, logic, rhetoric, mathematics, the sciences, various arts, literature, and philosophy. These and other subjects have been praised variously for their capacity to make us think; examine the limitations of our own knowledge; understand the rules of inquiry in its different modes; form habits of intellect that enable us to see connections that others might not; avoid parochialism and the idols of the tribe; examine matters at hand in terms of larger principles; reflect deeply on our own behavior in relation to the world around us; relate intellectual inquiry to the great moral and civic issues of the day; and use our wisdom to examine what constitutes the good life and to improve our own lives and those of others.

One need not buy into the faulty psychology underlying some of these arguments, or all the defenses of specific subject matter offered by the proponents of a liberal education over the years, to honor the perennial effort to define ends and approaches to teaching and learning that are not tied only to preparation for an occupation. If we understand the occupation of teaching to be the complex work I have been suggesting throughout this book, then a liberal education has value above and beyond its preparation of the teacher in the subject matter to be taught, or as a background for professional courses. For the teacher needs to be precisely the free and intelligent person that a liberal education seeks as its end.

Teachers from elementary school through college, no matter what other tasks they may be engaged in, ought to be occupied in the very enterprise of liberal education they have gone through themselves. We should take note of the fact that, unlike other occupations and professions, teaching seeks to carry on and reproduce the full person, to free the person to engage wisely in the great moral endeavor of life, and that teachers need to treat those they teach as ends in themselves. But of course the teacher is also a person, and the purpose of a teacher's

education cannot be limited to preparation to teach subject matter—
as, for example, Smith (1980) would have it: "It can hardly be overemphasized that the purpose of a preprofessional curriculum in pedagogy
is to prepare the prospective teacher in the subject matter he or she is
required to teach" (p. 32). Smith is here talking of the general education
of the student preparing to be a teacher. The sole purpose of the student's liberal education, for him, and for the authors of so many of the
recent documents in the teacher education reform movement, is to
produce a knowledgeable teacher. But what has happened to prospective teachers as ends in themselves? They are surely more than simply
conduits of knowledge. Otherwise, we have a rather crabbed conception of the teacher's own education as a kind of drudgery to master the
subject matter for the task of teaching it ahead. They are only instruments for the education of the young.

What if we were to view the teachers' liberal education, not as the
content of what they are going to teach, but as the inculcation of habits
of mind that enable us to lead our own lives wisely and contribute to
general moral progress? We would then have teachers who are not just
instruments to pass on subject matter, which they have learned for that
purpose, but wise persons who in the abundance of their knowledge
teach others, and teach them in ways that contribute to their becoming
persons, ends in themselves. Paradoxically, a liberal education works
best for teachers when its professional purposes are *not* in the fore-
ground of their own approach to learning, or in the purposes of *their*
teachers. Neither I nor any teacher with whom I have spoken claims
that the bulk of their own education took place in college or graduate
school. Lifelong learning is more than a slogan for teachers. We learn
as we prepare our classes and teach, as we reflect on our work with
others, as we read about what and how we teach. A liberal education
gets us started on that process of learning.

THE LIBERAL DIMENSION IN THE
PROFESSIONAL EDUCATION SEQUENCE

My celebration of a liberal education is in no way, as such celebra-
tions in the past often have been, accompanied by a disdain for a professional element in the preparation of teachers (Bestor, 1955; Koerner,
1963). The question is: How do we construe this professional element
in teacher education? Smith (1980) sees a professional school as one
whose "program focuses on the development of practical knowledge
and skills" (p. 11). What Smith and others are talking about are the

skills necessary for effective teaching in classrooms. They believe there is a body of knowledge about teaching and learning that can be translated into rules and prescriptions for teachers to follow, and that teachers in training can practice the implementation of these prescriptions at clinical sites. The call for such a focus is accompanied by a questioning of the sorts of research interests found among teacher educators with a graduate school mentality, and of the relevance of certain course work to the teacher's preparation:

> The basic program should be shaped by a single overriding purpose: namely to prepare prospective teachers for work success in the classroom, the school and the community. Every course should be scrutinized with respect to its contribution to this end. If this were done, a large number of courses would be eliminated at the level of basic preparation. Candidates for deletion would be introduction to education, history of education, philosophy of education, social foundations of education, and a host of others including courses in learning and development provided for in undergraduate study. (p. 40)

Now if the single overriding purpose of the school of education is to prepare teachers for work success in the classroom, the school, and the community, a great deal depends on how one defines the work of the teacher in those settings. It is not immediately apparent, as Smith and others would have it, that this work requires primarily the learning of prescriptions and practice in carrying them out. Smith reserves the philosophy of education and history of education courses for those in training to become school administrators or other kinds of specialists. I believe that he commits the administrative fallacy of believing that the real action in schools goes on in administrative offices, and that therefore those who would occupy such offices, making educational policies, need the broad educational background. I contend that the daily work of teachers in classrooms would also benefit from a broad liberal education.

I am not arguing here simply for the retention of what have come to be known as foundations courses in the curriculum. The argument I have been developing in this book is that, given my notion of the work of teachers, the best kind of "professional" program, whether at an undergraduate or graduate level, will contain a liberal perspective throughout. That liberal perspective should suffuse methods courses, student teaching, and the educative experiences that constitute the work lives of teachers.

For now, however, I want to note some understandable and/or legitimate aspects of Smith's concern with the lack of focus in profes-

sional teacher preparation. There is a tendency among teacher education faculty to become disseminators of fads and somewhat unthinking
responders to a variety of pressing concerns. As Smith (1980) asserts:

> When the faculty of pedagogy does not know what it is about, it grabs
> any and every new-fangled idea and purpose that any organization or
> agency offers, suggests, or insists upon. It will take on the task of providing
> courses, workshops or any other device for meeting such demands as the
> call to urban education, sex education, drug education, or human rela-
> tions education, even though the faculty is already falling far short of
> performing the task it was created to do: to train teachers in the knowl-
> edge and skills of classroom work. (p. 87)

Smith has run some diverse ideas together here, but his point has some
merit. Teacher education faculty do dissipate their energies, as well as
those of teachers and prospective teachers. I can think of no better
antidote to embracing fads, however, than a broad general education
for both the teachers and the teacher educators, one that includes an
understanding of appropriate processes of verification for whatever
claims may be made, and one that encourages sustained inquiry into
the purposes of the daily work of teaching and allows teachers to measure the latest "educational ideas" against these purposes.

The pressures are real ones. There is an anxiety about the schools
in our society, and a consequent desire to do something—anything—to
lessen the crisis. Hence we frequently hear statements like

> Educators must produce something that works and makes life more bear-
> able for teachers. They must help find ways of organizing schools and
> classes and of teaching students that are more effective. Such activities,
> however hard to realize, would reduce the barrage of charges against the
> educational institutions and their personnel. (Schwebel, 1989, p. 59)

I doubt that new ways of organizing schools and classes will be of
much help to the teachers. Nor do I believe that more effective teaching—a worthwhile end, to be sure—will come about as a result of new
techniques developed by either teachers or teacher educators. "Educators must produce something that works": This sort of language assumes
a view of useful knowledge about teaching as a set of cumulative products to be acquired by teachers and used in classrooms. The "product"
metaphor is perniciously misleading. Teacher educators and researchers
can make a contribution to the long-term education of teachers, but we
ought not to think that inventing techniques and handing them to the
teachers for implementation in the classroom is our major role.

Of course, well-educated teachers will be hungry for techniques that will help them plan, ensure order in class, and engage students more readily in the learning process. They will, however, view such techniques contextually. Are they appropriate to this group of students, to this subject matter and its purposes, to larger educational purposes? These kinds of assessments will be made wisely by teachers steeped in their subject matter and reflective about their work. One cannot dissociate the technical from the liberal in the education of teachers.

TEACHER EDUCATION AND THE GRADUATE SCHOOL MENTALITY

Some claim that teacher educators have been seduced by the graduate school mentality, with its emphasis on research. At the undergraduate level and for the many teacher educators who teach at the graduate level in institutions offering no doctoral work in education, this concern translates into a worry that the academic culture, with its emphasis on research and publication, has taken teacher educators from their more important tasks, teaching and service to the schools. Goodlad (1990) and many others question the emphasis on research among education faculties:

> In the flagship public universities there was little ambiguity: getting grants and publishing in high quality refereed journals was the name of the game. The change in focus from teaching to research, which evolved over the last fifteen or twenty years, was secure and accepted. Dissonance regarding preferred and perceived emphases was greatest for the older faculty members who had come when teaching and service were much more highly valued. Many viewed themselves as not respected by the younger "hot shots," who were well-prepared in research techniques; and the latter frequently observed that Professor So-and-so would not make tenure if evaluated today. (Goodlad, 1990)

Aside from issues of prestige and survival, which seem to dominate the literature about the place of teacher education in the university, the question arises whether there is any worthwhile relationship between the tasks of research and publication championed within the academic community, and the work of teacher education and the betterment of schools. I think the dichotomy set up between the graduate school study-of-education approach on the one hand and practical professional school training on the other vastly oversimplifies the issues at stake. There certainly are teacher education faculty members who do less research, inquiry, and writing because they focus on their teaching and service to the schools. It is also clear, especially in the research institutions, that many researchers have little interest in teacher preparation. But a lack of publications should not be taken as a guarantee that a faculty member is an excellent teacher or is to be found habitually working in the schools. Many faculty members find their teaching enhanced by their research interests. Some who don't do research or write about it are simply not very good at such tasks and, not surprisingly, tend to denigrate their worth.

Historically, the great research universities in this country developed with a more utilitarian and public-service orientation than the undergraduate liberal arts colleges, with whom they often found themselves in conflict. Leaders of the research university movement enunciated the idea of scientific inquiry for the public good. (The humanities have been uneasy with this model, and it is arguable that graduate work in the humanities is nothing more than professional preparation for college and university faculties.) Arguments have raged over the short- and long-term practicality and/or benefit to society of research in the natural and social sciences. But there is nothing anti-utilitarian about the graduate school ethos. Its very utilitarianism is precisely what created the tension between it and the proponents of a more general, liberal education. Researchers in the graduate schools of education who fail a fair test of relevance are not examples of the graduate school mentality; they depart from its utilitarian provenance.

The problem is not that the graduate schools are opposed to useful learning. The more substantive issue is: What shall be taken as useful by whom? Perhaps we ought to recognize that there will always be tension between practitioners and theorists, with the former tending to define usefulness too narrowly, and the latter too broadly. I would not, however, like to see the sort of sustained and sophisticated analysis of educational problems offered by a thinker such as Israel Scheffler, or the broad historical understandings of a Lawrence Cremin, or the debate among sociologists and economists about the extent to which schools contribute to social mobility, relegated to the sidelines by a narrowly construed notion of professional education. I suspect that a good part of the quality of the work of these scholars is traceable to their training in the academic disciplines they then bring to bear on schooling in our society. The time constraints on teachers and the seriousness of the problems with which they are faced too often lead them to dismiss difficult intellectual inquiries into educational issues as irrelevant to the teacher's work. But there are no short cuts in the business of teachers' educating themselves. I cannot point to any specific teaching behaviors that will result from teachers reading Schleffler, or Cremin, or the sociological debates about the role of schools in our society, but I am willing to wager that a teaching community whose members have a sophisticated awareness of the contexts in which they operate will, in the long run, be better off than one lacking in such understandings.

Dissatisfaction with the graduate school mentality and the recognition that it is enforced by hiring, tenuring, and promotion decisions has led some teacher educators to call for something approaching autonomy within the university. Thus Goodlad (1990) writes: "Programs for the education of educators must be autonomous and secure in their borders, with clear organizational identity, constancy of budget and personnel and decision-making authority similar to that enjoyed by the major professional schools" (p. 272). Smith (1980) argues that one of the hallmarks of a professional school is that its "program is designed without interference by other departments and schools" (p. 11). And Wiesniewski and Ducharme (1989) write:

> We insist on more autonomy for education units, autonomy to control admissions, set standards, prescribe curricula, and build on the liberal arts preparation of teachers. We are speaking here, of course, only to the structural relationship of a professional school to its university campus. (p. 153)

But there is some ambiguity here. The teacher education reformers, at their most thoughtful, are aware that there are intellectual benefits to be gained from the connection to the university.

> We do not advocate a return to normal schools. Even increased autonomy of education schools does not mean a retreat from the university culture. . . . The intellectual roots of teaching and learning are strongest on university campuses. Saying this in no way diminishes our commitment to collaboration with the practicing profession. (1989, p. 158)

There are understandable reasons why many teacher educators look to relative autonomy from the university to achieve gains, not the least of which are the short-sighted attitude toward the education of teachers on the part of too many of their colleagues in the liberal arts and the educators' own failure to take their role as educators of teachers as seriously as they take their role of preparing specialists for work other than teaching. I believe that these reasons do not outweigh the reasons for continued effort at cooperation, however difficult the process may be. Because of my understanding of the nature of teaching, I think it important that others besides professional educators have input into such issues as curriculum, research, and standards for faculty, and that teacher educators themselves participate fully in the shaping of the colleges and universities in which they work.

There are numerous good reasons for the continued effort at cooperation between teacher educators and others in the university. Fortunately, schools of education harbor both faculty and students who see themselves as revolutionaries or, more prosaically, agents of change. It would be surprising if the study of so central an institution of our society, and the prospect of working in it, did not attract missionaries and those filled with moral outrage. This happens in law and theology, in social work, and even in medicine. Jaroslav Pelikan (1992) argues that the university is best equipped to sustain this moral outrage within a context of concern with the fundamental intellectual virtues of "free inquiry and intellectual honesty" (p. 48). Neither the moral outrage nor the traditional virtues of the university should be denied. Newman (1976) argues that the university setting has a salutary effect on professionals and specialists. Outside, the professor "is in danger of being absorbed and narrowed by his pursuit." Inside the university,

> he is kept from extravagance by the very rivalry of other studies, he has gained from them a special illumination and largeness of mind, and freedom and self-possession, and treats his own in consequence with a philosophy and a resource, which belongs not to the study itself but to a liberal education. (pp. 145–146)

Finally, the liberal arts professors need the teachers and prospective teachers. Teaching the teachers forces them, as I argued in Chapter 6, to conceive of their own subject in its most liberal dimensions. It is difficult to keep channels of communication open between the school of education and the rest of the college and university. Seeking structural autonomy is not likely to help.

Status issues permeate the literature about teacher education and about the teaching profession. But decisions about how best to educate teachers, what sort of research needs to be done on the issues of education and schooling, what the connections of the researchers to the schools and to teachers ought to be, and the place in the university of schools of education, ought to be animated by something other than status concerns. Let us admit the bind in which we teacher educators find ourselves. By and large, other faculty in the university do not think well of us or the work we do. We are not likely to achieve widespread respect from them in the near future. Nor are we likely to achieve the kind of status we might if we were preparing individuals for a well-paid and prestigious profession such as law or medicine. Goodlad (1990) says: "Students in teacher education programs are aware and resentful of this low status, but they shrug it off, at least partially, as indicative of misplaced priorities in society and higher education" (p. 166). The students preparing to teach have greater burdens to bear than do the teacher educators. Goodlad spoke to groups of them about this issue:

> My question in group settings regarding the attitude of others always brought an outburst of giggles and a boisterous exchange of anecdotes. All participating had experienced reactions ranging from surprise to outright derision. Yet, their peers, in particular, ultimately came around to supportive, sometimes admiring views: "What you plan to do is needed and important," they said. "Someone must do it." (p. 201)

I think the students have it right. If society does not value our efforts, we will have to gain our sense of self-worth from the significance of the work we do, as we ourselves define it. So much depends on how we define that work. One can fight for salaries and better working conditions, and for increased competence in teachers and teacher educators. There is dignity in such fights. But one cannot argue effectively for one's own status in the eyes of others. Nor should one make decisions about the place of teacher education within the university based on such concerns. We are preparing teachers to carry on the great work of civilization. If we do it well, they will be working at the task of creating reflective individuals with the habits of mind necessary to identify and address the great moral problems of the next generation in a wise and competent fashion. I've found this a fulfilling way to spend my life.

9

THE PLACE OF SCHOOLS
IN THE EDUCATION OF TEACHERS

Educational reformers argue not only about the place of teacher education in the university but also about the role the schools themselves
ought to play in the education of teachers. Given the conception of the
work of teachers that I have been developing in this book, and the sort
of teacher education that would follow from such a conception, I want
to sketch out in this chapter the role that schools might play in that
education. I base my discussion on an understanding of John Dewey's
most fundamental thinking about education.

DEWEY'S ARGUMENT: RECONNECTING EDUCATION TO LIFE

When Dewey talks about learning, his major positive point is that
learning is life and growth. His negative corollary is that learning
should not be separated from the organism's daily life, its efforts to
survive and grow. Dewey argued that humankind had worked long
and hard at developing intelligent responses to the world and at shaping
the environment for its own ends. Those responses have enabled us to
live and grow, more specifically to clothe and house and transport
ourselves, and generally to survive and prosper. The knowledge and
skills acquired in human evolution became the funded knowledge of
the human race and, eventually, the content of the school curriculum.

The problem for the education of his day, in Dewey's eyes, was
that in formalizing this funded knowledge of humanity, in arranging it
in logical order, the textbook writers, curriculum makers, and teachers
had torn it from its roots as a set of responses to life's problems. They
had hidden from the students the fundamental purposes of the knowledge being taught. The Deweyan solution was to create schools in
which knowledge was reconnected to life, in which the links between
knowledge and the life of the individual and society were once again

made visible. Toward that end, the activities in the school for young children were to be closely correlated with those of the home. Dewey worried that the movement from an agrarian to an industrial society had left young people without the sort of vital work they had done on farms, "with a real motive behind and a real outcome ahead" (quoted in Dworkin, 1959, p. 37). On the farm, the connection between knowledge and life had been clear. Dewey, however, rejected nostalgia, recognizing that the emerging urban society had brought gains in flexibility and sophistication. He encouraged the school to become a small community, with students pursuing occupations and tasks within it. School was to become life, or as much like life as possible. The students' interest was to be captured by the real tasks addressed. Through work in the school community, the child would come to understand and reinvent the fundamental processes through which civilization had progressed. Dewey knew it was difficult for teachers to reconstruct reality in ways that would maximize its educative potential, and at the same time to retain the sense of real life that he considered so vital to the learning process.

What if we were to take Dewey's notion of the school as life and apply it to teacher education? The school, after all, is the work life of the teacher. My question is: To what extent can teachers render their work lives educative for themselves as well as their students? To what extent can the schools in which the teachers work become institutions in which the teachers learn as well as teach? The challenge for the progressive schools trying to educate children was to pattern the school experience as closely after real life as possible, to avoid the formalism, the artificiality, and the disconnection from life that Dewey saw as characteristic of most education in his own day. But when the school is considered as a locus of teachers' learning, then artificiality is not the problem; we find in the school real life in abundance. Like life everywhere, however, it can be, on the one hand, dull, or, on the other, overwhelming, and hence not educative for the teacher. The task for teachers is to reconstruct the life experience of the school so that it can educate.

In their work lives, teachers are doing things, as Dewey insisted learners should, with "a real motive behind and a real outcome ahead." That is a promising condition for learning. It ensures the learners' interest and subjects them to the discipline of necessary detail involved in a given task. Dewey's more general thinking about the conditions of learning is suggestive to those interested in creating schools in which teachers might learn, grow, and prosper.

DEMOCRATIC SPACES: DECISION-MAKING
AND TEACHER LEARNING

Following Dewey, teachers in such a school would have to form a democratic society. I do not mean this in a fuzzy or utopian sense. I mean simply that there would have to be large areas of their work lives about which the teachers could make decisions. Within the sort of school I am talking about, the avenues of communication are kept open, and teachers consult with one another and make decisions about the life of the school as well as life in their own classrooms. Dewey applauded the breaking down of hierarchical barriers in societies in which knowledge and decision-making had been the province of a particular class. He saw knowledge as becoming liquified, as infusing all of society. The democratic society was, for him, the educative society. It multiplied the avenues of communication within itself and sought to open up areas of communication outside itself.

The English Teachers

Let me try to illustrate Dewey's point about the democratic society's being a learning society. A committee of teachers whose members teach eleventh-grade English in a secondary school meets to choose a novel to include in the eleventh-grade curriculum. A suggestion that they establish criteria for their choice leads to a discussion in which the teachers comment on the interest displayed by their various students in the novels presently assigned. They move to conversation about the ways in which they handle each of the present readings. Some talk about their approaches in introducing each novel, others about specific writing assignments they have given. One teacher points out that with each novel she urges the students to note how authors reveal character through dialogue and action. Others report on classroom discussions in which they have explained how an author uses irony to advance a story or images to set a mood. Several say they try to relate issues in the novels to the lives of their students. One speaks of the importance of using literature to enhance vocabulary. The teachers begin to realize that there are similarities but also fundamental differences in their approaches to literature. Their argument over criteria for choosing a new novel, and their ensuing discussion over their methods of teaching the novels, reflect real differences in their purposes. Now perhaps one of the teachers will argue that the group has strayed too far from the task at hand: selecting a new book for the curriculum. But he would be missing the point of learning in a democratic society.

Let us look at what is going on here with our small group of English teachers. They have begun by following Dewey's model of inquiry. They have set a real problem for themselves; they have a real decision to make. They have begun to collect information. They recall levels of student interest in other novels. They recount their own approaches to teaching these other novels in order to establish what they think is worthwhile to teach, and from there to decide what new novel will likely be a good resource for their teaching purposes. They consider other information relevant to their choice. According to the Deweyan model of inquiry, they should next formulate a hypothesis. They might choose *Bleak House* as the novel best suited to their purposes in teaching literature to eleventh graders. The testing of the hypothesis would occur when the teachers taught the novel and discovered how well it suited their purposes.

But something went wrong with the Deweyan approach to inquiry here. That is why one teacher complained that they had strayed from their task. As they were collecting information to help them formulate their hypothesis, they began arguing over some of the information they were collecting. Clearly, how they treated other novels in their classes was relevant to the development of criteria for choosing a new novel, and hence to the eventual choice. But they discovered that they approached novels in quite different ways and that these methods or approaches reflected different understandings of their pedagogical purposes in teaching literature.

Even Dewey nods. His description of logical or scientific inquiry is often useful but sometimes misleading. Real-world inquiries are much messier and less linear, as we see with our teachers. In trying to solve one problem, the choice of a novel, they have opened up others. They become engaged in serious conversation about the how and the why, the purposes and methods of their daily work. The questions they are now raising are of no less significance, they are no less about the real world of their classrooms than the issue of which novel to choose. It is crackpot pragmatism to focus only on the task at hand when that task inexorably leads us to inquiries into the purposes and methods of our daily work. In this sort of wide-ranging discussion, the teachers learn that there are, in fact, many ways of approaching literature and arranging pedagogical priorities. In their interaction, the teachers gain the opportunity to see things from perspectives other than their own, to alter their own perspectives and ways of teaching, and to affect the ways in which others do their work. These possibilities for reciprocal learning occur because our teachers have cleared a democratic space within the school, one that gives them the opportunity to make real decisions about how and what to teach, and to do so after considering various perspectives learned in interaction with one another. They illustrate Dewey's point: "Knowledge is no longer an immobile solid; it has been liquified. It is actively moving in all the currents of society itself" (Dworkin, p. 37).

Let us return to our teachers. One urges that her colleagues read a book recently published by a literary critic, and that they identify the sorts of questions the critic asks about literature and adapt them for classroom use. Another reports on the approach taken to literature by a professor in the English department of a nearby university. A third suggests that the purposes of teaching literature to high school students differ radically from the ways in which literature is read by critics. He urges his fellow teachers to read a recent book by a philosopher of education that focuses on the purposes of citizenship and self-fulfilment in a humanistic education.

In Dewey's vision, a democratic society not only increased interaction within itself but also opened up channels to knowledge from outside itself. He believed that all waste in education was due to isolation. Here we see the teachers referring to and sharing readings and university experiences, but their interest is rooted in their classroom work, in choosing a novel for the curriculum, in rethinking their methods and purposes. The reading and other use of outside resources is done with professional concerns in mind: How ought I approach literature in my eleventh-grade classroom? What assumptions about teaching and literature have suffused my teaching? Do these assumptions hold up under critical inquiry? How will my new thinking about literature and teaching change the ways in which I introduce students to pieces of literature, the questions I ask my students, the writing assignments I give them? Not only will these teachers make a decision about a curriculum matter affecting their own work lives, they will re-enter their classrooms with insights gleaned in the discussion generated by their efforts to make the choice. The students will now have teachers whose understandings of literature and of their own teaching purposes have been enhanced by the inquiries they have undertaken.

Some might argue that the education of teachers within schools ought to focus on the daily workings of classrooms, on questions of classroom management, and leave to the university issues of educational purpose and subject matter expertise. There is some merit in this division of labor. Many classroom problems are most fruitfully discussed in the context of local conditions; a new teacher is more likely to receive immediately helpful advice about handling a difficult class from a wise old hand in the school than from a university class in educational psychology. At the same time, the school is not likely to harbor the sort of subject matter specialists and sustained inquirers into issues of educational purpose and practice that the university does.

But the merit of the argument goes only so far. In establishing an economy of teacher education, we err if we simply assign practical problems to the school and theoretical ones to the university. The theoretical and the practical have ways of becoming entangled, as we saw with the discussion on the teaching of literature. Many of the issues with which teachers are concerned in classrooms involve an intensification of inquiries begun within the teacher's general education, and an application and alteration of understandings achieved there. What is literature? What are the purposes of education? These are the sorts of questions one runs into in humanities courses in colleges. They take a unique and pressing form for English teachers teaching their subject to high school students, as similar questions do for teachers of other subject areas and grade levels.

Two things must be noted. First, those teachers whose minds have been captured by such issues in their general education are best prepared to reflect seriously upon them in the new forms they take in their classrooms. Reflection does not begin from scratch when teachers are faced with a problem. Both the habits of reflection and the understandings helpful to reflection on a particular issue have been accumulating as a part of the teachers' own general and professional education. Teachers bring more or less developed reflective capacities to the sorts of discussion described above. Second, the effort to intensify and apply the habits and understandings acquired by teachers in their general education reshapes and enhances those habits and understandings. So we cannot simply assign different parts of teacher education to different institutions. What we can do, in both the colleges and the schools, is maximize the conditions for learning and continue to explore the links between the two institutions. The interaction of teachers increases the reflective capacities of each teacher. Creating time and space for such interaction, organizing it intelligently, and linking it to school and classroom practice become crucial elements in developing a school in which the teachers as well as the students are being educated.

The Committee on Grading Practices

A school committed to democratic arrangements for teachers is a school in which teachers will be learning. Earlier in this chapter we analyzed a situation in which a group of English teachers met to choose a new novel for inclusion in the curriculum. This is the sort of activity

that one might find in many schools already—committees of teachers
working on some small alteration in the curriculum. Less frequently do
we find groups of teachers working on schoolwide policies. Let us look
at the educational benefits to a group of teachers who have taken on
just such a task.

The committee has grown out of a faculty member's concerns. He
has become anxious about his practice of grading his students more
strictly than other teachers of the same subject and at the same grade
level, fearing that his students—even though they might, in fact, as a
result of his class, be better prepared for college than other students—
are at a disadvantage when college admissions officers read their grades.
He has spoken to his department chair, to other faculty members, and to
the principal about this issue and found general concern among faculty
about various grading practices. The teacher becomes the head of a
committee whose purpose is to explore the issue of grading in the school
and to come up with recommendations for new grading policies.

At the first meeting of the committee, one teacher contends that
grading is the province of individual teachers and that no school policies
binding on teachers should be promulgated. The other members of the
committee disagree, arguing that they are all living in a school community and that it is necessary to develop consistent practices in areas such
as discipline and grading. Our teacher states again his concern about
his own strict grading in relation to what he perceives as his colleagues'
looser standards. A committee member argues that our teacher's standards are too harsh and discourage students from further effort. Another suggests that the importance of grading students lies in the fact
that students' grades tell them where they stand in relation to other
students in the class. Some members of the committee find this notion
disquieting, arguing that the school should not contribute to the general
competitive nature of the society and that grades should be viewed as
reports on how well an individual has mastered a certain definable
body of knowledge or improved over previous efforts at mastery.

At this point, the teacher who tried to call the English committee
back to its task of choosing a novel becomes furious. He urges the
committee to return to its task of drawing up a list of grading policies.
He announces that committees are a waste of time and that this is
positively the last one for which he will volunteer. Some of the teachers
agree that the discussion thus far has not been fruitful. One suggests
that they are dealing with a complex issue and that they should expect
initial forays into such issues to be frustrating precisely because of their
complexity. She adds that the grading issue is not merely a technical
one, since fundamental values are at stake. The teacher who had ini-

tially urged that individual teachers be allowed to make their own decisions about grading policy returns to the fray. Differences in these values, he argues, are precisely the reason why teachers should be left on their own in this matter.

The teachers on this committee have indeed taken on a complex set of issues. One of them, at the outset, has even questioned whether a common policy is appropriate in an area such as grading. Here, the committee and the school begin to grapple with the tension in American life between individualism and the effort to establish a community. Again, as with the questions of educational purpose raised by the members of the English department committee, we see a general issue taking a very specific form. The teachers do not argue over the academic question of the individual versus the community, but over what aspects of school policy ought to be formulated for the entire school community and what aspects should be left to the individual teacher — and why. The teachers have raised questions about the relationship of their grading to the outside world, to college admissions, and to the values of the society of which the students are a part. They have offered for discussion different perspectives from which grades might be viewed and have begun to realize what fundamental values are at stake in their discussion. Note again, however, that in-school education need not be confined to a "nuts and bolts" approach. Serious inquiry into nuts and bolts leads to questions about the purposes of the whole machine. And those questions of purpose gain a richness when they are embedded in the everyday life of the school.

Is there anything to be said for the position taken by the impatient teacher? Or is he a hapless foil in the march toward my argument's conclusion? The argument, and I think it is a sound one, is this: Schools, precisely because they are the work life of teachers, can be sites for the further intensification and application of a humanistic teacher education begun with broad general and professional course work. To further this education, democratic spaces must be cleared in schools, and conditions created in which teachers can share ideas with their colleagues, reflect on a variety of perspectives, and make decisions about the curriculum and other significant issues.

But let us grant a few points to our impatient teacher. First, some decisions have to be made; we cannot have endlessly branching inquiry when there is real work to be done. Second — and I understate the case — not all discussions are educationally fruitful for all participants. The quality of the discussions depends on the reflective capacities of the participants and their habits of listening and taking the points of view of others into consideration. Training in maximizing the learning potential of group discussions can be a help. Further, we need to acknowledge that the education of teachers, like the education of human beings generally, is a complex and continuous process, and that some new program or organizational strategy, or wider participation on decision-making committees, is not guaranteed to suddenly transform poorly educated teachers into wise participants in the life of the school.

The education of teachers within schools should be initiated and controlled by the teachers themselves. That initiation may take a variety of forms, from the seizure of decision-making power through teacher union pressure to the informal meeting of a small group of teachers to discuss shared classroom problems. Teachers should be wary of giving up their time for committee work that neither genuinely educates nor leads to real and significant decisions affecting their work lives. They should flee from such assignments. But surely no school is without colleagues willing to address significant issues in a reflective fashion and to work toward the implementation of decisions taken. School administrators would be wise to nurture democratic spaces in their school and to provide teachers who create them with financial and other support.

At least some of the impatience shown by teachers toward committee work is a product of the top-down, bureaucratic fashion in which teacher committees are formed and their purposes defined. Large urban school systems are particularly prone to this sort of approach. Individual schools receive from central administrators "guidelines" that may specify the composition of a committee: two supervisors, three teachers, one counselor, two parents, and so on. The guidelines ask the school participants to describe how they are going to meet a set of objectives already defined for them. They are to provide "timelines" and "action plans," to formulate "observable outcomes" and describe evaluation procedures. The wiser, older hands among the teaching staff run back to their classrooms, leaving the committees to the untutored arrogance of young idealists and the "practical" cynicism of the local administrators who, in the end, provide the higher-ups with the documentation they need to assure the real "powers that be" that something is being done. Producing such documentation becomes the focus of the committee's work, and the often significant issues at the root of the directives from the central office go unaddressed in any serious fashion. The educational possibilities inherent in a setting in which teachers working together focus on the real problems of the school are lost. Committees are useful only if the teachers involved are in on the formulation of goals. The educational merit of the teachers' experience lies in their efforts to alter goals in the light of their experience and to actively shape that experience in relation to goals. Teacher committees that meet these Deweyan criteria for learning and growth can be valuable.

OTHER WAYS OF LEARNING IN SCHOOLS

There are, of course, other ways in which contexts for learning can be created in schools. The interaction occurring in discussions among teachers concerning curriculum or other school policies can be extended to teachers visiting one another's classrooms. Our English teachers, for example, might want to enliven their discussion of different purposes in teaching fiction by seeing how these stated purposes are played out in different classrooms. Some will want to see just how the teacher who asserts the importance of the connection between literature and the lives of her students emphasizes that in her classroom. Perhaps two others have read together the approach of one of the literary critics they discussed and would like to emulate it in the sorts of questions they ask their students and in the assignments they develop. They might plan their classes together and observe each other's efforts, exchange feedback, and reformulate their classroom strategies. Such teacher learning can be extraordinarily energizing — can, in fact, bring new life to one's teaching. The teacher's experience, as Dewey would have it, is heightened and brought under conscious control by the observation and interaction. Top-down mandating of these sorts of activities undermines their educational purpose. The interactions must be teacher-initiated. Teachers must find colleagues from whom they can learn, whom they can trust to be supportive and honestly critical, and who themselves are open to new perspectives on their teaching.

Another approach to encouraging the education of teachers within schools, one much discussed in the recent teacher education literature, is journal writing. The keeping of journals forces reflection. Teachers keeping journals about their daily work set up a kind of objective interaction with the self. It is too easy to go through the weeks of a school year with vague thoughts about the quality of one's teaching, and with hazy promises to try new approaches when old ones are not working well. A teacher recognizes, for example, that a more detailed introduction to a particular reading the next time it is assigned would be helpful to the students, providing them with more context. But the impression, unless noted and returned to, is fleeting. Another example: A student's behavior in class is troubling. A journal provides the opportunity to form an objective picture of the behavior, consider its causes, and plan a new approach with the student. Or a teacher worries over his choice of teaching as a career. What does he find worthwhile and what negative in his day's work? What changes might be made in his work life to maximize its fulfilling aspects? Teacher journals may range over the whole life of the teacher. And, of course, they can be shared with others. Such journal-keeping follows Dewey's notion that the gap between raw experience and intellectual inquiry must be closed. The journal is a strategy for heightening the quality of the teacher's experience, for making it conscious and directed, rather than dull and overwhelming (Goswami & Stillman, 1987).

I can think of no better concrete inspiration for teachers wishing to reflect together on their own work in classrooms than Joseph McDonald's *Teaching: Making Sense of an Uncertain Craft* (1992). Using the metaphor of teaching as a text, he speaks of "reading" his teaching alone (through his journal) and with others (in conversations with teachers who are also reflecting on their work). The book sketches various aspects of this reading of teaching, emphasizing the uncertainty of the craft, in contrast to the notion that teacher behavior is governed by laws of learning devised by experts. The journal entries in the book, the teacher conversations, and the interpretations show intelligent and educated people wrestling with the complex problems of classroom life. This is how teacher knowledge is constructed.

When the teacher is the learner, the school itself turns out to be the real life with which Dewey felt the schools had lost touch. After all, the schools are the work lives of the teachers, places in which teachers do things "with a real motive behind and a real outcome ahead." The task of teachers and other school personnel is to make that life less routine or overwhelming, to reconstruct their experience so that it is brought under conscious control. Teacher committees working on real school issues, teachers visiting one another's classes, and the writing and sharing of journals are just some of the ways in which teachers have already begun to take charge of their own education. The construction of reflective experiences within schools ought not be viewed as an isolated part of the education of teachers. It is continuous with the teacher's university-based general and professional education. The habits of reflection and the significant issues raised in earlier parts of the teacher's education find specific applications in the school; they, in fact, enable teachers to define and alter that experience and to deepen and enlarge their own education. Teachers need time and space to reflect on their work lives.

10

School–College Collaborations

"Reforms worthy of the name are always slow; and reform even of governments and churches is not so slow as that of schools, for there is the great preliminary difficulty of fashioning the instruments—of teaching the teachers."
—John Stuart Mill (quoted in Garforth, 1971, p. 163)

In the preceding chapter, I was content to focus almost exclusively on a self-generated learning for teachers in schools. In this chapter, I would like to look at what happens when teacher educators themselves become involved in schools. Pity us poor teacher educators. At the university, we are seen by our colleagues in other fields as lacking a serious scholarly enterprise. If we turn to the schools for validation of the significance of our daily work, we find that the teachers perceive us as irrelevant, trafficking in unworkable theories and hopelessly cut off from the realities of school life. This unhappy situation has led us in two different directions: toward redefining our role in the university, and toward immersion in the real life of the school. What teacher educators, by and large, have not done is to strive for a thorough understanding of the nature of a teacher's work and, following on that, to fashion for ourselves a defensible role in response to that understanding.

I want first to look critically at the idea of large-scale school–college collaborations, and then to offer a more focused and limited form of cooperation as consonant with what I argue is a more legitimate role for teacher educators. The idea of such large-scale collaborations is almost universally praised within the teacher education community. In the heat of the commitment to work in the schools, however, few careful questions are asked about the role teacher educators might best play in schools and about the likelihood of their success.

131

THE WOODS ARE BURNING

Most of the literature about school–college collaboration (and it is a large literature) reflects a crisis mentality. The woods are burning. An immediate and massive response is necessary. Here is one such statement about the problems of our cities and schools, reflecting the substance and tone of many others: "Whatever else changes, the plight of the young of our cities has continued to stand as a national embarrassment through the sixties, the seventies and now into the eighties. . . . Enhancing opportunity for urban youth remains a largely intractable problem" (Mocker, Martin, & Brown, 1988, p. 42). Education, we are told, in the cities especially, is in disastrous circumstances. Teachers are demoralized; children are at risk. The dropout rate is unacceptably high; test scores are unacceptably low. None of this is exaggerated. These concerns are repeated over and over again as individuals report on the context and motivation that led them into school–college collaborations.

Mayors and urban school superintendents are under considerable pressure to show they are taking action in response to the problems of city and school. College presidents are also under pressure to show they are responsive to the problems of the cities and especially to those of public education. There is an inevitable political and public relations dimension to all of this. Large-scale, dramatic, eye-catching action is sought. Fortunately, pure motives are not necessary for the carrying out of beneficial enterprises. Teacher educators of intelligence and goodwill, with no political or public relations agenda, share the perception of crisis and seek to act in response to it. Their logic is this: The disarray in the schools is so great, and the consequence of this disarray for society so profound, that large-scale systemic changes are necessary in the school organization and, indeed, in the culture of the school itself.

What is sometimes not noticed is that, with the focus on large-scale change in school structures, the teacher educator's role expands. Added to the functions of inquirer and teacher is that of agent of change. We must now learn how to bring about institutional change. The focus, as Lieberman (1985) writes, is on organizational processes:

> How to make changes in schools that last: how to organize school improvement efforts, how to engage school faculties who have been refugees of many reform movements, and how to build and sustain commitment from school superintendents, principals, teachers and people in policy making positions at the state and national level. (p. 93)

An additional argument for structural change in the schools offered by teacher educators is that the present practices of the schools nullify the training new teachers receive in the colleges. Therefore, we have to create new sorts of schools that will support, rather than undercut, the preparation aspiring teachers have received. We need to create "exemplary sites" in which provisional teachers can continue to learn rather than have their learning undermined.

I want to offer a rather strong criticism of present large-scale collaborations between teacher education institutions and the schools, and to tender in its place what I think is a more defensible role for teacher educators in relation to the schools. In a crisis, a large-scale enterprise is seen by the reformers as the only appropriate response. But much of the talk about the reorganization and restructuring of schools has no real focus. It is an exercise in grandiosity that, I suspect, is rooted in teacher educators' sense of homelessness, of being lost somewhere between the school and university cultures, somewhere between thinking and doing. It is the same loss of a sure sense of purpose that leads us to so much worry about the place of teacher education within the university.

The restructuring of any organization is likely to have educational dimensions. But when teacher educators become involved in such restructuring, it seems fair to say that they are focusing on producing particular organizational changes, not on educating teachers. They have stepped out of their role as educators in any ordinary sense of the word. My argument is not that teacher educators should never step out of this role, but that when they do, they should recognize that they are no longer in the role for which they have been trained. They are going about a quite different task — call it management, or organizing, or diplomacy — and very few are likely to bring with them the same sorts of abilities, derived from original interest, training, and experience, that they bring to their work as educators. Many of the people who give an organizational tilt to these projects are themselves college administrators or former school administrators. They are doing what they are drawn to, by interest, talent, and experience, and perhaps a little anxious hubris.

THE FAILURE OF ORGANIZATIONAL UTOPIANISM

I find no basis in history or in good sense for the belief that colleges should be the initiators and sustainers of large-scale reforms in schools. Speaking of the idea of exemplary schools growing out of large-scale school–college collaboration, John Goodlad (1990) says, "There are not yet models operating at a level worthy of emulation—a condition of great usefulness to reform efforts" (p. 282). Goodlad goes on to tell us that, nevertheless, such school–college collaboration, in which schools are renewed and become appropriate places for the education of teachers, is an idea whose time has come. Given the absence of models worthy of emulation after more than two decades of efforts, it might make sense to ask why no such models exist, and whether a fundamental reappraisal of the way in which colleges relate to schools is not in order.

The larger collaborations begin in the minds of political leaders and school and college administrators. At their best they represent plans to solve far-reaching social problems. They are defined, not by limited efforts to alter certain teaching approaches in a particular subject area, but by larger ends toward which the educational or political leaders hope to lead the schools and society. Look, for instance, at 3 of the 11 goals that Goodlad (1990) has included in his agenda for the fictional Susqua Valley School–University Partnership—goals 1, 4, and 9:

> (1) The development of school curricula that reflect the very best analyses and projections of what young people need in order to be effective citizens, workers, parents, and individuals. . . .
>
> (4) The restructuring of schools to ensure sequential, integrated learning in the most important domains of knowledge and knowing; a drastic reduction in students' alienation; a substantial increase in the personalization of learning in more familylike groupings; and establishment of an atmosphere of fairness to all—of human decency, if you will. . . .
>
> (9) The creation of exemplary teaching sites in which future teachers are educated—sites that demonstrate both the best we know about how schools should function and the best we know about how to maintain them in a renewing mode. (p. 326)

Read through these goals a second time. They have a limitless, dizzying quality. Most of them strike me as criteria any of us involved with school practice and policy ought to keep in mind as we go about our work. But as an agenda for school change they are hopelessly utopian, utopian in the sense that they begin outside present historical realities, outside the concrete and specific struggles in which teachers and teacher educators are already involved. They illustrate the utopian management fallacy, the belief that institutions can be created and planned from scratch, and that the task of the participants is to deduce from the outlined principles an assortment of implementing activities.

Look for example at Goodlad's first item, on curriculum design, or what should be taught. Teachers are in classrooms already, teaching a certain subject matter. They are heirs to a history of curriculum change in their own subject area and to wider historical arguments about school purposes. It is wise for them to reflect from time to time on the worth of what they are doing. But such reflection will arise from and be bounded by the historical development of their subject matter and by the concrete teaching tasks in which they are immersed. Teachers, thank heaven, do not decide on curriculum matters by asking what the latest "projections and analyses" say is likely to produce good workers, citizens, and so forth. Kliebard's (1986) historical study of the arguments over curriculum in the American high school should be mandated reading for those who would design curriculum in this way.

Not all efforts at large-scale organizational change suffer from this unfocused grandiosity. Here is an example of an effort that I think falls halfway between the sort of large-scale efforts I find objectionable and the approach I think most worthwhile. I asked one college faculty member, a longtime and sensible participant in school–college collaborations, what he thought was the most important change that had occurred in a school in which he had been deeply involved over a number of years. He answered that it was the school restructuring which had been accomplished several years after the collaboration had begun. The school had been divided into smaller units, allowing for more sustained contact among teachers who regularly discussed interdisciplinary aspects of the curriculum, and for regular guidance classes and mentoring of individual students. This faculty member argued against what he called limited projects with limited goals, against incremental changes not having any long-term effects.

Here the reorganization into smaller units is clearly stated as a goal. It took a long time to accomplish, my informant tells me, but it seems to be having worthwhile results. At least some of the teachers are using the time allotted to discuss ways in which their various subjects might be integrated for their students, and this activity itself is likely to have educational value. But the quality of the interaction among the reorganized teachers will, of course, vary, depending in large part on the sort of education the teachers involved have had. It is on this educational element that I think we should be focusing, rather than on organizational factors.

I suspect that organizational arrangements that seem so important as they are being planned and implemented are, in the long run, more evanescent and less educationally significant than the long-term, hard-won educational development of teachers. Of course, it is important that schools be organized so that teachers have time to interact. The schools do not need teacher educators to inform them of that. But perhaps too much of the literature on school collaborations focuses on organizational arrangements. Speaking in a different context, John Wilson (1980) has said that "it is somewhat as if books and magazines under the heading 'chess' were to be devoted mostly to the administration of chess competitions rather than to the game itself" (p. 46).

None of this is an argument against teacher educators' being involved in schools. There are good reasons why they should be. Schools are the places, after all, where the activities they are inquiring into and teaching about go on. The question is: What sort of work should they be doing there? I am not arguing here that teacher educators can be drawn to the schools if we allow them to pursue their private interest, research and publication, for which they will be rewarded with tenure and promotion. My argument is of a different sort. The roles that teacher educators have developed over the years are those of (1) making inquiries into teaching, schooling generally, and education in a larger sense, and publishing the findings and understandings derived from these inquiries, and (2) teaching — specifically, teaching prospective and working teachers. These functions seem valuable. They should not easily be discarded or diminished.

There is much argument over the quality and content of each of these functions, and a great deal of fuss over which of them should take priority. I think that each is unexceptionable. It seems only good sense that the teacher educator's work in the school be an implementation of one or both of them. In Goodlad's *Teachers for Our Nation's Schools* (1990), he distinguishes between teacher educators' offering "ad hoc services" to the schools and "effecting change" in them. His example of an ad hoc service is "a faculty member's response to a school's request to review the research on student grouping patterns" (p. 179). There is a categorizing mistake in his distinction between teacher educators' providing ad hoc services to the school and effecting change there. The distinction is used to support his argument that preferable to piecemeal efforts on the part of teacher educators are large-scale planning, covering all aspects of a school, and implementation of such planning in organizational changes. But, obviously, one can at least contribute to changes in a school by performing ad hoc services. In the example offered, a university faculty member is asked to review the research on grouping of students. Presumably, the school is reconsidering its own grouping policies and wishes to find out something about what has happened in other school districts that have adopted various grouping policies. The inquiry they have asked the researcher to make places him in a position to at least participate in effecting change in the district.

But Goodlad and many others opt for school–college collaborations on a much grander scale. They tend to dismiss an ad hoc or service orientation in the relationship of universities to schools. The problems of the schools are so huge, they argue, that they require large-scale organizational planning and change. A second argument, and one to which I am more sympathetic, is that university people ought not to provide small services to badly working institutions, because the services tend to be swallowed up — that is, distorted by the priorities of the school. There is some truth in this argument, but I think it does not necessarily hold for changes that are the product of a genuinely educational relationship between teacher educators and teachers. If a group of teachers working with a college representative has come to understand a new approach to the teaching of some aspect of their subject area — if they have tried it and refined it, and evaluated it — they will certainly incorporate it into their teaching repertoire for some time to come. Other kinds of changes, changes that do not involve the education of teachers (for example, the introduction of some new practice without the full understanding of the teachers involved in it) are less likely to survive.

AN ARGUMENT FOR SMALLER, FOCUSED PROJECTS

Let me make a positive argument for small-scale interventions. Many teacher educators find themselves spending some time in schools during each semester. Typical activities are the supervision of student teaching (or some other form of fieldwork) and working with individuals or small groups of teachers to implement new curriculum approaches. Let us say a mathematics teacher educator begins talking to a few teachers in the math department in a local school where she is supervising two student teachers. They discuss new approaches to teaching mathematics proposed by the state education department. The math educator has previously served on the state committee that formulated the proposal. The teachers, including the chair and the teacher educator, find the discussions worthwhile and interesting, but time-consuming. They are impressed with the teacher educator's mastery of the new approach. The teacher educator learns a great deal about the real problems of implementation faced by the teachers. Moreover, her discussions with the teachers deepen her understanding of the place of mathematics education in the general education of young people, an issue in which she has a long-standing if inchoate interest. The discussions lead to a decision to apply for a grant from the state education

department. The grant will involve, among other things, graduate summer courses taught by both the math educator and a member of the
mathematics department at the university, open to teachers from the
department in question and to teachers and department chairs from
neighboring school districts. It will also involve observations by the
teachers, workshops assessing classroom efforts and suggesting alterations in approaches, and teachers teaching their fellow teachers.

This is a small-scale enterprise focused on one subject area, not on
a whole school or school district. It has little public relations value in
times of urban crises. It does not promise to turn the schools around. It
is not a desperation touchdown pass; but it does seem likely to grind
out a few yards. The teacher educator is engaged in teaching. She is
respected for her expertise. She has something very specific to offer,
and the teachers respect her for it. And she is learning from them.
Observing and conversing with them, she learns what she could not
have learned without being present and working in this school. She is
learning about the changes that must occur in curriculum and teaching
ideas as they encounter the realities of classroom life. These are lessons
that increase her own store of wisdom about theory and practice, about
teachers and students, and about curriculum and classroom interaction.
Toward the end of the project, she will publish an article on one aspect
of it that will be co-authored by two of the teachers whose interest and
talent led them to this closer collaboration. Because of her involvement,
she becomes better at what she does: teaching about and inquiring into
the teaching of mathematics to secondary school students.

The teachers are learning, too. They wanted to know more about
a new approach that affects both the content and the methodology of
what they teach. They are mastering the approach, placing it in the
context of what they know about mathematics and teaching. They have
opportunities to try out new teaching ideas and to reflect on them with
other teachers, with the teacher educator, and with a more theoretical
mathematician from the university. In a later phase of the project some
of them will be involved in the teaching of in-service courses. Both the
teacher educator and the teachers benefit from this enhancement of
their understanding of related issues beyond the identified scope of the
project. In what genuinely educational contexts does this not happen?

Note that the project is initiated in an interaction between teachers
and a teacher educator, and that it is about a very specific issue of
interest to both parties. One does not begin with the idea of a large-
scale collaboration, move to the articulation of a set of long-range goals,
and then try to deduce school practices from them. We begin in the
midst of the teachers' work, the teaching of mathematics. There is

an organic quality to the enterprise. Projects that extend the teacher educator's functions of teaching and inquiry into the school, that draw on his or her expertise, that grow out of the needs and interests of both the teacher and the teacher educator, and that are clearly defined at an early stage of involvement are likely to meet with some success.

I see the ebb and flow of school and other institutional change as plural, halting, and tentative, and I see human intelligence as at its best when making smaller meanings within larger structures, experimenting, reformulating not-too-distant goals and moving toward them. The argument with my claim is, of course, the one with which we began: that current educational problems are so unwieldy that massive organizational change within schools is needed. I agree with the diagnosis but question the prescribed cure. School organizational changes are, for the most part, like quicksilver. I am not suggesting that some organizational changes might not benefit the education of young people in schools. They do, insofar as they enhance the life of teachers and students in classrooms. But intelligent organizational changes are more likely to flow out of needs perceived in focused teacher projects than out of contractual arrangements arrived at by school superintendents and college administrators. The sheer distance from the locus of the educational act — the place where learning occurs — of the school–college collaboration planners as they enter into multidistrict contracts and as they set up national advisory councils, task forces, commissions, and centers for the study of this or that aspect of education, should warn us that these projects are not likely to enhance the education either of teachers or of their students. The exchanges between teachers and students are at the heart of the school enterprise, and it is these exchanges that ought to be the bull's-eye at which teacher educators aim in their work in schools.

John Stuart Mill attributed the slowness of the reform of schools to "the great preliminary difficulty . . . of teaching the teachers" (quoted in Garforth, 1971, p. 163). We cannot skip over that difficulty by focusing on questions of the organization of schools. Teaching the teachers is a large and difficult task, one worthy of our sustained commitment. We can carry it on in schools as well as in college classrooms.

AFTERWORD

Perhaps, I think as I put this book to bed, I am fighting a straw man. Many of my colleagues in teacher education and most of the teachers already agree with me. But in the late summer of 1993, I receive an issue of *American Educator*. It is the national magazine of the American Federation of Teachers, and copies are mailed to every single one of its dues-paying members. In bold type filling up the entire cover are these two sentences: "Teaching methods based on research in cognitive science are the educational equivalents of polio vaccine and penicillin. Yet few outside the educational research community are aware of these breakthroughs or understand the research that makes them possible" (Bruer, 1993).

So it's not a straw man. This limited view of the nature of teacher knowledge and its implications for teacher education is still very much with us. The quotation is taken from the lead article in the issue, by John Bruer. The article reviews the research of cognitive psychologists into how experts approach problems differently from novices, and how this research has been applied in classrooms. The research reported is really fascinating. Teachers ought to be aware of it. They should digest it. They should bring their own energies and interests to it. They should not merely acquire it, but approach it philosophically and see how it fits in with their previous knowledge, their present purposes, the subject matter they teach, and the students with whom they work, and how it might be altered for their own use. What they should not do is see it as the educational equivalent of a wonder drug. Does anyone really believe that we now have the "educational equivalents of polio vaccine and penicillin"? This is not just a medical analogy. This is fantasy— fantasy fueled by a longing to right the myriad wrongs of the school with a scientific discovery. Research to the rescue! And all the teachers will have to do is familiarize themselves with the research and the practice based on it.

I have argued that the work of the teacher is such that professional preparation should be more a deepening and a specification of the content and approaches of a general liberal education than a pursuit of a separate knowledge base similar to that needed by medical doctors and engineers. Indeed, I believe that this knowledge base metaphor, rooted as it is in concerns about status, has badly skewed the ways in which we think about teaching and teacher education.

We must surrender the notion that teachers can be trained in workshops to respond to contemporary educational concerns such as multiculturalism with a specific set of behaviors. We must, instead, educate our students broadly and well, and trust that they will be able to apply the perspectives gained in a broader education to whatever problems confront them in classrooms. The only behavior we ought to specify for teachers graduating from our teacher education programs is that they go on pursuing their education.

REFERENCES

Anderson, J. (1988). Cognitive styles and multicultural populations. *Journal of Teacher Education, 39,* 2–9.

Ayer, A. J. (1936). *Language, truth and logic.* New York: Dover.

Banks, J. (1988). Ethnicity, class, cognitive, and motivational styles: Research and teaching implications. *Journal of Negro Education, 57,* 452–466.

Banks, J. (1993). Multicultural education: Historical development, dimensions, and practice. In L. Darling-Hammond (Ed.), *Review of* Research in Education (pp. 3–49). Washington, DC: American Educational Research Association.

Bell, D. (1966). *The reforming of general education: The Columbia College experience in its national setting.* Cambridge, MA: Harvard University Press.

Bennett, W. (1986). *To reclaim a legacy: A report on the humanities in higher education.* Washington, DC: National Endowment for the Humanities.

Berliner, D. (1987). Knowledge is power: A talk to teachers about a revolution in the teaching profession. In D. Berliner & B. Rosenshine (Eds.), *Talks to teachers: A festschrift for N. L. Gage* (pp. 3–33). New York: Random House.

Bernstein, R. (1978). *The restructuring of social and political theory.* Philadelphia: University of Pennsylvania Press.

Bernstein, R. (1983). *Beyond objectivism and relativism: Science, hermeneutics, and practice.* Philadelphia: University of Pennsylvania Press.

Bestor, A. (1955). *The restoration of learning.* New York: Knopf.

Bloom, B. (Ed.). (1956). *Taxonomy of educational objectives. Handbook 1: Cognitive domain.* New York: McKay.

Borrowman, M. (1956). *The liberal and the technical in teacher education: A historical survey of American thought.* New York: Bureau of Publications, Teachers College.

Borrowman, M. (Ed.). (1965). *Teacher education in America: A documentary history.* New York: Teachers College Press.

Bowles, S., & Gintis, H. (1976). *Schooling in capitalist America.* New York: Basic Books.

Bredo, E., & Feinberg, W. (Eds.). (1982). *Knowledge and values in social and educational research.* Philadelphia: Temple University Press.

Bruer, J. T. (1993). The mind's journey from novice to expert. *American educator, 17*(2), 6–15, 38–46.

Bruner, Jerome. (1960). *The process of education*. Cambridge, MA: Harvard University Press.

Carin, A., & Sund, R. (1989). *Teaching science through discovery*. Columbus, OH: Merrill.

Carnegie Forum on Education and the Economy. (1986). *A nation prepared: Teachers for the twenty-first century*. New York: Carnegie Corporation.

Chinn, E. (1979). Cultural values and motivation. (Fact sheet). Reston, VA: ERIC Clearinghouse on Handicapped Children.

Clifford, G. J., & Guthrie, J. W. (1988). *Ed school*. Chicago: University of Chicago Press.

Darling-Hammond, L. (1988). Accountability and teacher professionalism. *American Educator, 12*, 8–13, 38–43.

Dewey, J. (1950). *Reconstruction in philosophy*. New York: New American Library.

Dewey, J. (1964). *Democracy and education*. New York: Macmillan. (Original work published 1916)

Driver, R. (1986). *The pupil as scientist?* Philadelphia. Open University Press.

Dunkin, M. J., & Biddle, B. J. (1974). *The study of teaching*. New York: Holt, Rinehart & Winston.

Dworkin, M. (1959). *Dewey on education*. New York: Teachers College Press.

Education for Democracy. (1987). *A statement of principles: Guidelines for strengthening the teaching of democratic values* (A joint project of the American Federation of Teachers, the Educational Excellence Network, and Freedom House). Washington, DC: American Federation of Teachers.

Erickson, F. (1986). Qualitative methods in research on teaching. In M. Wittrock (Ed.), *Handbook of research on teaching: A project of the American Educational Research Association* (3rd ed.; pp. 119–161). New York: Macmillan.

Fenstermacher, G. (1986). Philosophy of research on teaching. In M. Wittrock (Ed.), *Handbook of research on teaching: A project of the American Educational Research Association* (3rd ed.; pp. 37–49). New York: Macmillan.

Fitzgerald, F. (1979). *America revised: History schoolbooks in the twentieth century*. New York: Vintage.

Gage, N. L. (1978). *The scientific basis of the art of teaching*. New York: Teachers College Press.

Garforth, F. (Ed.). (1971). *John Stuart Mill on education*. New York: Teachers College Press.

Gay, Geneva. (1986). Multicultural education in Western societies. In J. Banks and J. Lynch (Eds.), *Multicultural education in Western societies* (pp. 154–175). New York: Holt, Rinehart & Winston.

Goodlad, J. (1990). *Teachers for our nation's schools*. San Francisco: Jossey-Bass.

Goswami, D., & Stillman, P. (1987). *Reclaiming the classroom: Teacher research as an agency of change*. Upper Montclair, NJ: Boynton Cook.

Grant, G. (1988). *The world we created at Hamilton High*. Cambridge, MA: Harvard University Press.

Grimmett, P., & Erickson, G. (1988). *Reflection in teacher education.* New York: Teachers College Press.

Gutmann, A. (1987). *Democratic education.* Princeton, NJ: Princeton University Press.

Holmes Group. (1986). *Tomorrow's teachers: A report of the Holmes Group.* East Lansing, MI: Author.

Houston, W. R. (Ed.), Haberman, J., & Sikula, J. (Assoc. Eds.). (1990). *Handbook of the association of teacher educators.* New York: Macmillan.

Hutchins, R. M. (1936). *The higher learning in America.* New Haven, CT: Yale University Press.

Isaac, J. (1987). *Power and Marxist theory.* Ithaca, NY: Cornell University Press.

James, W. (1981). *Pragmatism.* Indianapolis: Hackett.

Jarolimek, J. (1977). *Social studies competencies and skills: Learning to teach as an intern.* New York: Macmillan.

Jencks, C. (1972). *Inequality: A reassessment of the effect of family and schooling in America.* New York: Harper.

Johnson, H., Jr. (1980). *The public school and moral education.* New York: Pilgrim Press.

Judge, H. (1982). *American graduate schools of education: A view from abroad.* New York: Ford Foundation.

Katz, Michael. (1971). *Class, bureaucracy, and schools: The illusion of educational change in America.* New York: Praeger.

Kliebard, H. (1986). *The struggle for the American curriculum: 1893–1958.* New York: Routledge and Kegan Paul.

Koerner, J. D. (1963). *The miseducation of American teachers.* Boston: Houghton Mifflin.

Kuhn, T. (1962). *The structure of scientific revolutions.* Chicago: University of Chicago Press.

Kuhn, T. (1977). *The essential tension: Selected studies in scientific tradition and change.* Chicago: University of Chicago Press.

Lieberman, A. (1985). School improvement: Common sense, common knowledge. In S. Packard (Ed.), *The leading edge* (pp. 93–104). Washington, DC: American Association of Colleges of Teacher Education.

Lortie, D. (1975). *Schoolteacher.* Chicago: University of Chicago Press.

MacIntyre, A. (1981). *After virtue.* Notre Dame, IN: University of Notre Dame Press.

Manicas, P. (1987). *A history and philosophy of the social sciences.* Oxford: Basil Blackwell.

Maritain, J. (1943). *Education at the crossroads.* New Haven, CT: Yale University Press.

Mayhew, K. C., & Edwards, A. C. (1936). *The Dewey school: The laboratory school of the University of Chicago, 1896–1903.* New York: D. Appleton-Century.

McCarthy, R., Skillen, J., & Harper, W. (1982). *Disestablishment a second time: Genuine pluralism for American schools.* Grand Rapids, MI: Christian University Press.

McDonald, J. (1992). *Teaching: Making sense of an uncertain craft*. New York: Teachers College Press.

McKay, N. (1987). Reflections on black woman writers: Revising the literary canon. In C. Farnham (Ed.), *The impact of feminist research in the academy* (pp. 174–187). Bloomington: Indiana University Press.

McQuade, D. (Ed.). (1981). *Selected writings of Emerson*. New York: Modern Library.

Miller, J. (1987). Teachers' emerging texts: The empowering potential of writing in-service. In J. Smythe (Ed.), *Educating teachers: Changing the nature of pedagogical knowledge* (pp. 193–205). Philadelphia: Falmer Press.

Mocker, D., Martin, D., & Brown, N. (1988). Lessons learned from collaboration. *Urban Education, 23*, 42–50.

National Commission on Excellence in Education. (1983). *An open letter to the American people. A nation at risk: The imperative for educational reform*. Washington, DC: U.S. Department of Education.

Newman, J. H. (1976). *The idea of a university*. (Ed. with introduction and notes by I. T. Ker). Oxford: Clarendon Press.

O'Connor, D. J. (1966). *An introduction to the philosophy of education*. London: Routledge and Kegan Paul.

Pelikan, J. (1992). *The idea of the university: A reexamination*. New Haven: Yale University Press.

Phenix, P. (1964). *Realms of meaning: A philosophy of the curriculum for general education*. New York: McGraw-Hill.

Pieper, J. (1952). *Leisure: The basis of culture* (A. Dru, Trans.). New York: Pantheon.

Plato. (1974). *Republic* (G. M. A. Grube, Trans.). Indianapolis: Hackett.

Popper, K. (1959). *The logic of scientific discovery*. New York: Harper.

Proefriedt, W. (1980). Socialist criticisms of education in the United States. *Harvard Educational Review, 50*, 467–480.

Proefriedt, W. (1981). The significance of the teacher's work. *Educational Theory, 31*, 341–349.

Rodriguez, R. (1982). *Hunger of memory: The education of Richard Rodriguez*. New York: Bantam.

Rosenshine, B., & Stevens, R. (1986). Teaching functions. In M. Wittrock (Ed.), *Handbook of research on teaching: A project of the American Educational Research Association* (pp. 376–389). New York: Macmillan.

Scheffler, I. (1965). Philosophical models of teaching. *Harvard Educational Review, 35*(3), 131–143.

Scheffler, I. (1983). The moral content of American public education. In H. Giroux & D. Purpel (Eds.), *The hidden curriculum and moral education* (pp. 309–317). Berkeley, CA: McCutcheon.

Schlesinger, A., Jr. (1991). *The disuniting of America: Reflections on a multicultural society*. New York: Norton.

Schön, D. (1983). *The relective practitioner: How professionals think in action*. New York: Basic Books.

Schön, D. (1987). *Educating the reflective practitioner: Toward a new design for teaching and learning in the professions.* San Francisco: Jossey-Bass.

Schwebel, M. (1989). The new priorities and the education faculty. In R. Wiesniewski & E. Ducharme (Eds.), *The professors of teaching: An inquiry* (pp. 52–66). New York: State University of New York Press.

Shanker, A. (1985). *The making of a profession.* Washington, DC: American Federation of Teachers.

Sichel, B. (1988). *Moral education: Character, community and ideals.* Philadelphia: Temple University Press.

Skinner, B. F. (1967). *Walden two.* New York: Macmillan.

Sleeter, C., & Grant, C. (1987). An analysis of multicultural education in the United States. *Harvard Educational Review, 57,* 421–444.

Smith, B. O., with Silverman, S., Borg, J., & Fry, B. (1980). *A design for a school of pedagogy.* Washington, DC: U.S. Department of Education.

Stock-Morton, P. (1988). *Moral education for a secular society.* Albany: State University of New York Press.

Twentieth Century Fund. (1983). *The report of the Twentieth Century Fund task force on federal secondary and elementary policy.* New York: Author.

U.S. Department of Education. (1986). *What works: Research about teaching and learning.* Washington, DC: Author.

Vesey, L. (1965). *The emergence of the American university.* Chicago: University of Chicago Press.

Wiesniewski, R., & Ducharme, E. (Eds.). (1989). *The professors of teaching: An inquiry.* New York: State University of New York Press.

Wilson, J. (1979). *Fantasy and common sense in education.* Oxford: Robertson.

Wilson, J. (1980). Philosophy of education: Retrospect and prospect. *Oxford Review of Education, 6,* 41–52.

Wittrock, M. (Ed.). (1986). *Handbook of research on teaching: A project of the American Educational Research Association* (3rd ed.). New York: Macmillan.

Zevin, J. (1992). *Social studies for the twenty-first century: Methods and materials for teaching in middle and secondary schools.* White Plains, NY: Longman.

Altruism, of teachers, 100–103
American Educator, 141
American Federation of Teachers, 67, 141
Anderson, J., 72–73
Ayer, A. J., 12, 14

Banks, J., 74
Behaviorism, 5, 14–20
  appeal of, 14–16
  and behaviorist-empiricist approach,
    16–22
Bell, Daniel, 42
Bennett, William, 38
Berliner, David, 4, 95–96, 98, 102
Bernstein, R., 14
Bestor, A., 112
Biddle, B. J., 4
Bloom, Benjamin, 80–82, 87
Borrowman, Merle, 5, 47, 108
Bowles, S., 20–21
Bredo, E., 14
Brown, N., 132
Brown v. Board of Education of Topeka,
  63
Bruer, John T., 141
Bruner, Jerome, 41–42, 82

Career orientation. *See also* Professional-
    ism, of teachers
  and liberal arts education, 39–40, 42–43
Carin, Arthur, 80–82
Carnegie Forum on Education and the
    Economy, 101, 104
Certification programs, 4
Chinn, E., 73–74
Civil rights movement, 11
*Class, Bureaucracy, and Schools: The Illu-
    sion of Educational Change in
    America* (Katz), 20
Clifford, G. J., 1–2

Community
  and democratic approach to learning,
    122–129
  Plato on, 58–60
  and professionalism of teachers, 103–107
Competency-based teacher education
    (CBTE), 4
Cremin, Lawrence, 108, 110, 116
Cuban, Larry, 1–2
Curriculum
  liberal arts, relativism of, 38–42
  and moral education, 65–71
  and multicultural education, 71–78

Darling-Hammond, Linda, 94
Democratic education, 122–129
  and committee on grading practices,
    125–129
  of English teachers, 122–125, 129
Dewey, John, 5, 11–12, 44–46, 88–93,
    120–124, 129, 130
Differential staffing, 96–97, 99, 103–107
Divinity schools, curriculum of, 44
Doherty, Bill, 10
Driver, Rosalind, 82
Ducharme, E., 117
Dunkin, M. J., 4
Dworkin, M., 121, 124

Economic determinism, 21
Educational Excellence Network, 67
Educational purpose
  and questioning, 84
  of teacher education, 56
Education for Democracy, 67
Edwards, A. C., 90
English, democratic approach to teaching,
    122–125, 129
Erickson, F., 22
Erickson, G., 98

Feinberg, W., 14
Fenstermacher, Gary, 32
Finn, Chester, 23
Fitzgerald, F., 77
Flanagan, John, 9
Freedom House, 67

Gage, N. L., 4, 17–19, 22, 28
Galen, 3
Garforth, F., 131, 139
Gay, Geneva, 71
Gintis, H., 20–21
Goodlad, J., 107, 115, 117, 119, 134–135, 136–137
Goswami, D., 130
Grading, committee on practices in, 125–129
Grant, C., 73
Grant, G., 66
Grimmett, P., 98
Guthrie, J. W., 1–2

Haberman, J., 5
Harper, W., 70
Harrington, John, 10
Harvard College, 39, 40
Hermeneutics, defined, 22
Hirsch, E. D., 26
Holmes Group, 96–97, 99, 103–104
Homer, 55
Houston, W. R., 5
Hutchins, Robert Maynard, 43–45

Inequality (Jencks), 20
Isaac, J., 21
Isolation, of teachers, 32–34

Jacobs, Hayes, 25
James, William, 15
Jarolinek, John, 81
Jencks, C., 20
Johnson, H., Jr., 70
Journal writing, 129–130
Judge, Harry, 108

Katz, Michael, 20
Kliebard, H., 77, 135
Knowledge, of teachers, 95–100
   concept of, 96
   and differential staffing, 96–97, 99, 103–107

general and specialized, 99
and other professions, 98–99
and teacher education, 97–98
Koerner, J. D., 112
Kuhn, T., 22

Lead teachers, concept of, 104
Learning styles, and multicultural education, 72–75
Learning theory, of Dewey, 88–93
Liberal arts education, 36–48
   and career orientation, 39–40, 42–43
   and curricular relativism, 38–39
   development of persons as purpose of, 110–112
   and mind/body dualism, 43–45
   philosophical text in, 49–62
   and professionalization, 40, 112–115
   and reflective approach, 36–38, 45–48
   and search for unified curriculum, 40–42
   and specialization, 40
Liberal model of education, 5–6
Lieberman, A., 132
Lortie, Dan, 32–33

McCarthy, R., 70
McDermott, John, 11
McDonald, Joseph, 130
MacIntyre, A., 66
McKay, N., 76
McQuade, D., 16
Mangan, Tom, 9
Manicas, P., 98
Maritain, Jacques, 47
Martin, D., 132
Marxism, 21
Mathematics, school-college collaboratives in, 137–139
Mayhew, K. C., 90
Methods of teaching, 79–93
   democratic approach, 122–129
   Dewey on, 88–93, 122–124, 129–130
   questioning, 80–88
Mill, John Stuart, 131, 139
Miller, Janet, 34
Mocker, D., 132
Modeling, of teaching on writing, 25–35
Moral education, 65–71
   arguments about, 68–70
   core beliefs in, 67–68

Plato on, 60–61
  and religion in schools, 70–71
  technical vs. liberal approach to, 66–67
Multicultural education, 71–78
  and curricular changes, 75–77
  and learning styles, 72–75

National Commission on Excellence in Education, 22
Neill, A. S., 26
Newman, John Henry, 36, 51, 61–62, 118
New School for Social Research, 25

O'Connor, D. J., 12

Pelikan, Jaroslav, 118
Performance-based teacher education (PBTE), 4
Phenix, Philip, 12, 41
Philosophical text, in teacher education, 49–62
Pieper, Josef, 43, 47
Plato, 37, 48, 49–62, 84, 102
Popper, K., 14
Positivist approach, 14
Process-product research, 4, 16–19
Proefriedt, W., 21
Professionalism, of teachers, 94–107
  and altruism, 100–103
  collegium in, 103–107
  and knowledge, 95–100
  and liberal arts education, 40, 112–115
Progressive education, 64–65

Questioning, 80–88
  and Bloom's taxonomy, 80–82, 87
  and educational purpose, 84
  and nature of subject, 82–84
  and understanding of self, students, and the world, 84–88
Quinn, John, 9

Raywid, Mary Anne, vii–ix
Reflective approach, 7–24
  and altruism, 102–103
  and behaviorist approach, 14–20
  and behaviorist-empiricist approach, 16–22
  deepening process in, 21–22
  and democratic approach, 125

and first-year teachers, 8–10
and formal inquiry, 12–15
informal conversations in, 9–12
journal writing in, 129–130
and liberal arts education, 36–38, 45–48, 112–115
and new conservatism, 22–24
philosophical text in, 49–62
and questioning, 84–88
and structuralism, 20–21
writing compared to teaching in, 25–35
Religion, in schools, 70–71
Republic (Plato), 48, 50–62
Rodriguez, R., 74–75
Rosenshine, B., 29
Rowe, Mary Budd, 82

Scheffler, Israel, 12, 67–68, 116
Schlesinger, Arthur, 76–77
Schön, Donald, 98–99
School-college collaborations, 131–139
  crisis mentality in, 132–133
  large-scale, problems of, 132–137
  small, advantages of, 137–139
Schooling in Capitalist America (Bowles and Gintis), 20
Schools
  as democratic spaces, 122–129
  differential staffing of, 96–97, 99, 103–107
  as life, 120–121
Schwebel, M., 114
Scientific Basis of the Art of Teaching, A (Gage), 17–19
Shanker, Albert, 94, 100, 104–105
Sichel, B., 68
Sikula, J., 5
Skillen, J., 70
Skinner, B. F., 16
Sleeter, C., 73
Smith, B. Othanel, 108, 112–114, 117
Social Studies for the Twenty-First Century (Zevin), 81
Socrates, 3, 13, 37, 39, 61–62
Soltis, Jonas, 12
Sophocles, 37, 46
Specialization, and liberal arts education, 40
Stevens, R., 29
Stillman, P., 130
Stock-Morton, P., 77

Structuralism, 20–21
  and school-college collaborations, 132–139
Sund, Robert, 80–82

Teacher education
  and altruistic presumption, 101
  complaints about, 1–4
  democratic approach in, 122–129
  educational purposes of, 56
  ferment in, 34
  "imposter" phenomenon in, 1–2, 3–4
  journal writing in, 129–130
  and knowledge, of teachers, 97–98
  "no progress" phenomenon in, 1–3
  philosophical text in, 49–62
  questioning methods in, 80–88
  role of, in university, 115–118
  rules of, 28–30
  and school as life, 120–121
  and school-college collaborations, 131–139
  technical approach to, 28–30
Teachers College, Columbia University, 12
Teachers for Our Nation's Schools (Goodlad), 136
Teachers' unions, 11, 67, 141
Teaching
  isolation in, 32–34
  technical proficiency in, 30–32

as uncertain profession, 26–30
  writing process compared to, 25–35
Teaching: Making Sense of an Uncertain Craft (McDonald), 130
Twentieth Century Fund, 22

U.S. Department of Education, 23
Utilitarianism, and liberal arts education, 39–40, 42–43

Vesey, Lawrence, 39
Vocationalism, 39–40, 42–43

What Works: Research About Teaching and Learning, 23–24
Wielunski, Ziggy, 9
Wiesniewski, R., 117
Wilson, Harry, 10
Wilson, John, 97–98, 99–100, 136
Wittrock, M., 5
Writing
  isolation in, 32–34
  teaching compared to, 25–35
  technical proficiency in, 30–32
  as uncertain profession, 26–30
"Writing Across the Curriculum" course, 34

Young, Tom, 9, 10

Zevin, Jack, 81

ABOUT THE AUTHOR

A former high school English teacher, **Bill Proefriedt** has been a teacher educator at Queens College for 25 years. He has been chair of the department of Secondary Education there, and has also taught courses in the Philosophy department and in the American Studies Program. His articles have appeared in *Teachers College Record, Educational Theory, Education Week, Newsday,* and in many other places.